Indo-Tibetan Studies Series : 1

TIBETAN STUDIES

PAST AND PRESENT

Editor

Narendra Kumar Dash

Kaveri Books

New Delhi-110 002

ISBN: 978-81-7479-039-2
Edition 2017

Published by
Kaveri Books
4832/24, Ansari Road
New Delhi-110002 (India)
Tel: 011-23288140, 23245799
E-mail : kaveribooks@vsnl.com
kaveribooks@gmail.com
Website: www.kaveribooks.com

Typeset at
Delta Book World, New Delhi - 110 002

PRINTED IN INDIA

VISVA-BHARATI

FOUNDED BY

RABINDRANATH TAGORE

ACHARYA
INDER KUMAR GUJARAL
UPACHARYA
DILIP KUMAR SINHA

• विश्वभारती •
शान्तिनिकेतन

SANTINIKETAN—731 235
WEST BENGAL, INDIA

Foreword

Indo-Tibetan Studies have long been a feature of Buddhistic studies programme at Visva-Bharati. Professor Sylvain Lèvi, the first Visiting Professor of this University, took personal care for the promotion of researches on Buddhism at Santiniketan, particularly on comparative aspects. He encouraged young scholars to learn not only the Sanskrit and Pali originals of the Buddhist literature but also to be acquainted with the respective translated versions in Tibetan and Chinese. After the departure of Prof. Levi (1922) from Santiniketan, Buddhist studies were taken up in our University by Prof. Vidhusekhara Bhattacharya, Prof. Tan Yun Shan, Prof. G. Tucci, Prof. P. C. Bagchi and many other erudite scholars. It is sheer through assiduity of Prof. Bhattacharya, the Tibetan Studies established itself as a separate discipline and several scholars, from India and abroad, had gathered to study Tibetan language and Tibetan Buddhist texts under his supervision. Tibetan Lamas were also invited to this sacred place of Gurudeva to assist the Indian scholars. Subsequently through the untiring efforts of Dr. P. C. Bagchi the Department of Indo-Tibetan Studies was established in 1954. This Department is an unique centre for studies on Tibetan Buddhism and Indo-Tibetan cultural relations, in the setting of Indian higher education system. No other University has possibly a post graduate department for the study of Tibetan language and literature in India.

I am happy to know that the Department is publishing the research papers, contributed by profound scholars in the national seminar on 'Tibetan Studies: Past and Present', in the form of book. I hope this volume will be attractive for scholars from India and abroad and it will be hopefully an asset to the academic world.

DILIP K. SINHA
Upacharya

Editorial

Cultural intercourse between India and Tibet started after the establishment of Buddhism in Tibet. A sixteen member delegation, headed by Thon-mi-sam-bhota, the minister of the great King Srong-btsan sgam-po of the Tibetan royal empire, visited India to learn Indian language and scripts in the mid-seventh century A.D. Indians like Padmasambhava, Kamalasila and many other erudite scholars visited Tibet and propagated the religion and philosophy of Lord Buddha. They have also translated Sanskrit Buddhist works into Tibetan. After Padmasambhava, a number of Tibetan monks visited India, studied at Nalanda and Vikramasila and went back to their home to give their countrymen the fruits of their study. Thus, Indian Buddhism exercised considerable influence over the Tibetan Buddhism in the literary and philosophical spheres. The Tibetan art, architecture, education, dance, drama, and even agriculture was influenced by the Indian systems. Besides the Buddhist works, the Tibetan also translated the secular Indian works on art, architecture, lexicon, poetics, medicine, law, grammar and Sanskrit literature into Tibetan. Almost all the translations have been preserved in the Tibetan canon. Tibetans made the translations in a scientific way. Not a single work has been translated into Tibetan single handed. They have always taken the help of the Indian scholars for an accurate and word to word translation of the Sanskrit originals. In the 8th century A.D., a committee was constituted for the standardization of the translated works which were completed earlier. They also composed a dictionary type of work containing the original Sanskrit technical words of Buddhist religion and philosophy and allied words and their Tibetan equivalents. The work called the *Mahavyutpatti* was used by the subsequent translators as a hand book to remove the ambiguities regarding some basic and key terms. Some of the Lo-tsa-bas also have consulted the Chinese translation of the respective works to remove their doubts on some difficult passages. Thus the translation of the Indian works into Tibetan was very systematic.

Though the Buddhist Sanskrit texts attracted the notice of the Chinese scholars in the Second century A. D. onwards, still the Tibetans made most outstanding contributions through preserving the Sanskrit texts in literal and accurate translation, in which they surpassed the Chinese in accuracy and volume. Thus the Tibetan language contains the richest collection of Buddhist literature in the world today and all aspects of the Buddhist tradition—*Hinayana, Mahayana,* and *Vajrayana* are contained within its scope.

Tibetan Studies in India

In the modern times the devoted Hungarian scholar, Csoma de Koros, continued the ancient tradition of Indo-Tibetan studies and brought them out of the speculation of specialized learning into the open field of world scholarship. Jaschke and Franke also worked hard in this field and Jaschke's *Tibetan-English Dictionary* may be regarded as the first on scientific lines. In Bengal, S. C. Das's Dictionary may still found indispensable to scholars of Tibetology. The Sanskrit-Tibetan studies were also given a big hand by Pandit Rahula Sankrtyayana in the thirties of this era. He discovered about five hundred Sanskrit Buddhist texts in the various monasteries of Western and Central Tibet and those works have been preserved in the K. P. Jayaswal Research Institute at Patna.

So far as the publications of the Tibetan works in India are concerned the Tibetan type for printing is available in India easily after the arrival of the Tibetan scholars in India. The International Academy of Indian Culture, founded by Dr. Raghuvira and promoted energetically by his able son Dr. Lokesh Chandra, has been publishing a series of important books. A similar series of Tibetan works with erudite introduction by Gene Smith has also been published from Delhi. At Varanasi, the Sampurnananda Sanskrit Visva-Vidyalaya and the Central Institute of Higher Tibetan Studies are taking keen interest nowadays in restoration of works from Tibetan into Sanskrit. The Institute of Tibetology, Gangtok and also the K. P Jayaswal Research Institute, Patna are also deserve special mention for their collection of works. Above all the Library of Tibetan Works and Archives at Dharmasala under the guidance of H. H the 14th Dalai Lama is promoting and propagating Tibetology in India since its inception.

The Tibetan Institution at Ladakh and Sarnath provide necessary training in theory and practice to the Lamas on Tibetan Buddhism. Although these Institutions are established on the traditional Tibetan pattern, they are also providing modern technical knowledge. For the development of Tibetan Studies in India, some teachers for language and literature have been appointed in the Universities of Delhi, Banaras, Allahabad, Lucknow, Nagpur, Gorakhpur, Kurukshetra, Calcutta, Chandigarh and Shimla and instruction in Tibetan is being given in schools of Foreign Languages at Delhi; Dalhousie; Pachmari, Khadak-Vasla near Pune etc.

Tibetan Studies at Visva-Bharati

Realising the importance of the Tibetan language for the study and research on ancient Indian culture and literature,

Gurudeva Rabindranath Tagore, introduced the learning of Tibetan Language at Visva-Bharati at the early twenties of this era. His main aim was "to bring into more intimate relations with one another through patient study and research, the different cultures of the East on the basis of their underlying Unity". To fulfil this very object, Professor Sylvain Levi joined Visva-Bharati as a Visiting Professor in 1921. Professor Levi's erudition scholarship and wide outlook attracted scholars and young learners and they became enthusiastic in learning Tibetan and Chinese alongwith Sanskrit, Pali and Apbhramsa to explore the hidden treasure of the Indian Culture in general and Buddhism in particular. His discourses on the Indian culture with reference to Buddhism had a great impact upon the then Ashramites of Santiniketan. A new trend thereby developed to study Buddhism from different prospective, with the help of the Tibetan, Chinese, Sanskrit & Pali languages.

After the departure of Prof. Levi, Prof. Vidhusekhara Bhattacharya carried out the studies on Tibetan Language and Literature and scholars from all over India and abroad had assembled to study this language under his supervision. They were also engaged in researches in various aspects of Buddhism. For a better understanding of the Tibetan texts and to remove some ambiguities during the study of independent Tibetan commentaries, traditional Tibetan Lamas were also invited to assist the Indian Scholars. By this way Visva-Bharati became a leading centre for Tibetan studies not only in India but also in the world. Finally Dr. Bagchi took over the responsibility and by his untiring efforts the Institute of Indo-Tibetan Studies was established in 1954 with the financial help from University Grants Commission with the following objects:

1. To promote systematic study and investigation of Indo-Tibetan Cultural relations down the ages;
2. To arrange for study of Tibetan culture in general and Tibetan Buddhism in particular;

3. To restore old Sanskrit texts preserved in Tibetan translations;
4. To make Tibetan texts available in translated version both in Indian and foreign languages;
5. To promote research in the Indo-Tibetan field through exchange of information with other cultural and scientific bodies in India and abroad engaged in similar research;
6. To publish monographs containing results of study and research undertaken by the students of the Institute;
7. To train Tibetan scholars in the study of Sanskrit and Pali texts and Sanskrit scholars in study of Tibetan texts;
8. To provide for a course in Classical and Modern Tibetan leading to a Certificate of Proficiency followed by advance course leading to a Diploma in the same subject;
9. To establish a Research Library and Museum to cover the Indo-Tibetan Studies field.

Presently this is the only Post Graduate centre in the Indian Universities for the learning of Tibetan language and literature, except CIHTS, Sarnath. The Department organised a two day national seminar at Santiniketan on "Tibetan Studies: Past & Present" in 1998. Leading Indo-Tibetologists of India were participated and contributed their research papers in the Seminar. The said papers have been published in this Volume for the benefit of the scholars, researchers and those who are interested in this field. I presume this Volume will be accepted widely by the academicians and others.

I am grateful to the authorities of our University for the financial assistance to organise the Seminar. The Director and staff members of Burdwan School of Computers and the proprietor of Kaveri Books and his team deserve special thanks as without their active co-operation it would not have been possible to publish the book.

Narendra Kumar Dash

Santiniketan

Contents

Foreword *iii*

Editorial *v*

1. Indo-Tibetan Studies at Santiniketan: Past and Prospects by *Biswanath Banerjee* 1
2. A Glimpse on the Tibetan Language Studies by *Suniti Kumar Pathak* 6
3. Buddhism in Tibet: An Overview by *Pranabananda Jash* 19
4. Personal Observations on Tibetan Language and Literature by *Lama Chimpa* 37
5. Lepcha Studies and Some Social Values Evaluated by *Arpita Chatterjee* 43
6. A Glimpse of the Tibetan Lexicography by *Kalpika Mukherjee* 48
7. Tibetan Language in Three Decades (1960-1990) by *Anandamayee Ghosh* 55
8. Contribution of Guru Padmasambhava on Spread of Buddhism in Sikkim by *Dechen D. Dorjee* 61
9. Role of Padmasambhava in Tibet by *Bela Bhattacharya* 69

10. Mask: A Significant Trait of the Tibetan Culture by *Chittaranjan Patra* 76

11. Non-Violence and Nature Awareness in the Chos kyi tsi gs su bcad pa (Dhammapada) by *Malavika Bandyopadhyaya* 84

12. An Analysis of the Authentic Authorship of the Tibetan Medical Treatise "Cha lag bco brgyad" (12th Century A. D.) and a Description of its Historical Background by *Barbara Gerke* 90

13. Tibetan Language and the Council in Standardization by *Jampel Kalden* 119

14. Prof. Tucci's Work in the Field of Buddhist Logic by *Heramba Chatterjee Shastri* 123

15. Hetutattvopadesa: A Study by *Narendra Kumar Dash* 129

16. Relation Between Sanskrit and Tibetan by *Biplab Kumar Mondal* 146

17. Buddhist System of Education by *Prakriti Chakraborty* 153

18. The Ran-Bshin Gsum-la jug-Pa'i. Sgrub-Pa of Arya Nagarjuna: A Critical Study by *Lalita Chakraborty* 165

Contributors 198

Index 201

Indo-Tibetan Studies at Santiniketan: Past and Prospects

1

Biswanath Banerjee

The tradition of modern Tibetological research was practically found in India by the Hungarian scholar Alexander Csoma de Koros when his untiring activities in the field bore fruits in the publications of illuminating and revealing Papers and Memoirs in the *Journal of Asiatic Society of Bengal.* The tradition was successfully followed up by the great scholar-explorer Sarat Chandra Das. Facing enormous difficulties and hardship Sarat Chandra Das saw Tibet personally with the eye of an inquisitive observer and from the knowledge of an earnest scholar. Besides his valuable Papers on Tibet and Tibetan culture published in different Journals of the time his monograph entitled Indian Pandits in the Land of Snow is a document like work revealing Tibet in a new light. His monumental work of the compilation of a *Tibetan-English Dictionary* published in 1902 has remained unsurpassed even now, and is a must for any serious student of Tibetan to collaborate with. In spite of these pioneering activities Tibetology was not a popular subject of study and was confined to only a few. There was no serious and scientific arrangement for a systematic study of Tibetology in the country. Gurudeva Rabindranath realised the importance of research and higher training in Tibetan studies and invited scholars including learned Lamas to come to his *Ashrama* and engage themselves in fruitful academic pursuits. He was convinced of the importance and relevance of Tibetan studies, along with a study of Sanskrit, Pali and Prakrit, for the discovery of our past. But in the early thirties of this century Santiniketan had not sufficient resources to make a provision for a systematic training and research in Indology and Tibetology to act according to the ideals of Gurudeva. Individual scholars, however, undertook researches in the line and made notable contributions.

The fore-sight of an academic-administrator like Sir Asutosh Mookerjee also realised the necessity of Tibetan studies and took steps making adequate arrangements for Tibetological studies in the University of Calcutta. Valuable Tibetan Xylographs and other source-materials in Tibetan were collected and a learned Tibetan was appointed to help Indian scholars. We cannot fail to remember the very important and voluminous work by Mahamahopadhyaya Satish Chandra Vidyabhusana on the history of medieval Indian Logic, published in 1920. The volume was prepared with materials collected from a large number of works on Logic in Tibetan. Besides this great work the University of Calcutta published some very important books with Tibetan materials, like Ksemendra's *Bodhisattvavadana-kalpalata* by Sarat Chandra Das, Dharmakirti's *Nyayabindu* and Dharmottara's commentary on it by Stcherbatsky, Nagarjuna's *Mula-madhyamaka-karika* by La Vallee Poussin, and many other similar texts of great importance. For, the learners of the Tibetan language Mahamahopadhyaya Vidhusekhara Sastri prepared an excellent Tibetan Chrestomathy entitled *Bhota-Prakasa* in 1939. It cannot be denied that in the study of Tibetology Bengal and Calcutta have given a lead to the rest of India. The Asiatic Society of Calcutta, the University of Calcutta and the Visva-Bharati are the three prime institutions in the country to take to the study first and now we have a number of Institutions in almost every part of India for higher training and research in Tibetology.

With this background of Tibetan studies in the country a full fledged Department of Indo-Tibetan Studies was founded at Santiniketan in 1954 with two teachers under the supervision of Prabodh Chandra Bagchi. The nomenclature of the Department is significant from academic and cultural point of view. It is not a Department to impart lessons in Tibetan language and literature only, certainly it should be mainly occupied with the task of studying the close relation that has been existing between India and Tibet since historic times. The Department is expected to promote a systematic study and investigation of Indo-Tibetan cultural contacts down the ages.

Indo-Tibetan Studies have been an important feature of the Buddhistic Studies programme in Vidya-Bhavana even before the enactment of the Visva-Bharati as a Central University.

A systematic and scientific study and investigation in Sino-Indian and Indo-Tibetan cultural relations virtually started at Santiniketan when on the invitation of the Poet the great French savant Professor Sylvain Levi joined the institution in 1921. Professor Levi took particular care that Buddhistic studies at Santiniketan should be broad-based and should draw upon, particularly on the comparative side, not only the Sanskrit and Pali originals but also the translated versions in Chinese and Tibetan. Under his inspiring guidance Indian scholars were trained in Sinology and Tibetology on a scientific line. Young scholars were assembling at Santiniketan to study Tibetan with Sanskrit and Pali originals. A complete collection of Tibetan classical literature and other source-materials were collected. Over the years a large number of volumes and manuscripts have added to the bulk of the library. Promising scholars assembled at Santiniketan and there was a great tide of academic pursuits centring China, Tibet and India. At different times scholars like Mm. Vidhusekhar Sastri, Prabodh Chandra Bagchi, Dhramadhar Rajaguru Mahasthavir, Phanindra Nath Basu, So Nam nGo Dhruba, Ngo Cheong Lim, V. Lesny, Sten Konow, N. Aiyyaswami Shastri, Shanti Bhikku Shastri, Sujit Kumar Mukherjee, Walter Liebenthal, Muni Jinavijayaji and a few others worked here, each with a definite project and published important texts and original Papers as if to give a shape to the ideas of Gurudeva. One of the earliest publications of this period was Nagarjuna's *Mahayana-vimsaka*, a Sanskrit text reconstructed by Vidhusekhara from Tibetan and Chinese versions and published in 1931 with an English translation. Vidhusekhara worked on a number of such texts one after the other and we have from him the reconstructed Sanskrit text of Aryadeva's *Catuhsataka* from Tibetan version with an English translation, Asanga's *Yogacarabhumi, Nyayapravesa* of Dinnaga, and many others on various subjects. The text of *Nairatmya-Pariprccha* was discovered by Professor Levi and Sujit Kumar Mukherjee reconstructed the text on the basis of Tibetan in 1931. He also prepared the texts of *Sardulakara-navadana,* Asvaghosa's *Vajrasuci, Asokavadana* etc. The texts of *Karatala-ratna, Bhavasankranti-sutra, Alambana-pariksa, Dvadasmuha-sutra* etc. exhibit the quality of the painstaking research of N. Aiyyaswami Shastri. The versatile Italian scholar Prof. Giuseppe Tucci worked at Santiniketan for some time and the preparation and publication of the text of *Madhyanta vibhaga sutrabhasyatika* of Sthiramati was the result of his collaboration with Vidhusekhara. It is not that all these works prepared by scholars at Santiniketan were published by the Visva-Bharati.

Even after the demise of Gurudeva this type of research and training continued at Santiniketan for quite sometime in the Department of Chinese, Philosophy, Sanskrit, Pali & Prakrit with Shanti Bhikkhu, Sukhamay Saptatirtha,

Liebenthal, Venkataraman and a few others, but slowly this spirit of doing something new or the urge to bring to light something unknown, has disappeared! It is unfortunate that since the creation of a separate Department for the subject no sincere attempt has been made to keep up the glorious tradition of the institution. Much energy has been spent to run the language courses, but in this sphere also the number of students has gone decreasing! It is not that there has been a dearth of talents or want of facilities for research, what is needed is an inspiring guidance that will set the Department to the right direction. It cannot be expected that students will throng around the Department, but the members of the Department have to justify their existence. The infrastructure for Indo-Tibetan studies at Visva-Bharati is indeed encouraging. The Library is well-equipped and there is a rich collection of manuscripts, both Sanskrit and Tibetan. The members in the Department should be inspired with the idea to set examples by their own sincerity and activity! There is a real prospect to activise the Department by undertaking original research on the basis of unpublished materials, restoration and reconstruction for Sanskrit texts lost in originals, translation of Tibetan texts into English or Indian languages, particularly of those Tibetan texts which have preserved the lost Sanskrit originals, and so on. But this type of work is not that easy. Persons undertaking such works should be properly equipped with good knowledge of Sanskrit and Tibetan, as also should be conversant with the technique of doing this type of work. Learned Tibetan Lamas with good knowledge of Sanskrit must be made available to the Department for collaboration. Aims and objects with which the Department was created may serve as the guidelines to achieve success in reviving the Department and restoring the past glory of the institution.

I wish the members all the best in their attempt.

A Glimpse on the Tibetan Language Studies

2

Suniti Kumar Pathak

Language Geography of Tibetan

As usual, the boundaries of language geography of Tibetan is wider than her ethnic localities.[1] The geomorphic Tibet consists of the following major divisions, *Stod bod*, *Smad*, *mdo-kham*. The *Yar klungs* valley[2] became prominent since the Btsan rulers who established their stronghold by the six century A. D. At the same time Nyari 'khor sum including Guge and Purang flourished prior to the introduction of Buddhism in the seventh cent. A. D. from Nepal and China.

The Btsan principalities settled in the *yar klungs* had became powerful in militia and their commercial expansion was led by the traders of *mdokham* and *Stod bod* upto the 10th century A. D. in the neighbouring countries like, Liyul (Khotan) and adjacent city states of Central Asia like *Khasgar*, Karasar, also China and Nepal[3]. Again, the Tibetan speech extended in the adjoining areas due to extensive commercial progress in Szechuan, Gansu, Uighur in northwest China, Xin hai, Mongolia and Manchuria. Furthermore, the Tibetans migrated and settled in the Indian Himalayas.[4]

Moreover, the Buddhists of Tibet had a wide access in the neighbouring countries China, Mongolia and Central Asia,

Bhutan, Sikkim and the Indian Himalayas. In course of cultural diffusion of Buddhism the Tibetan language had also included many loan words from speeches spoken by those neighbouring countries. [5]

Genesis of Tibetan

According to the Chinese records of the pre-T'ang period, the inhabitants of Hsi fan (Tibet) were *kiang* shepherds and nomadic peoples who had a pastoral livelihood.[6] Probably, the Chinese authors of those days were not adequately informed about the Bon po ritualists of the southwestern Trans-Himalayan region. Prior to the advent of Bon po practitioners, the ancient 'Brog pa habitants of the Trans-Himalayan had indigenous speech traits in different ravines of the hills.

The Bon po records[7] claim that the early migration of the Bon practitioners occurred by the 4th century A. D. from *stag gzig* (east Iran) to Guge through *Bru zha*, which might be the Gulgasth area, present day Gilgit. However, the Bon po inherited an indigenous culture stratum which had been distinct from that of the Avestan of the ancient Iran.

Modern scholars like Namkhai norbu[8] claim that the speech of *Stod bod,* presently named Tibetan, generated out of composite speech genera in which various elements of nomadic speech traits had been mixed along with those in the ancient *Bon po* speech. A large number of unagglutinated monosyllabic dictions may go in support of that view. Several bilingual (Tibetan and Zhang zhung) texts which come down along with the *Zhang Zhung* bilingual dictionary have opened a new approach.[9] Moreover, the *Dun Huang* cave materials in Tibetan and the Tibetan documents collected from Chinese Turkestan[10] leave a room to review the question of the genesis of Tibetan. Monosyllabic semblance of Chinese and Tibetan may not be the only criterion to uphold the common view of like Sino-Tibetan Speech Family among the Asian languages.[11] For instance, the Korean language is not an offspring of Japanese in spite of their geographical affinity in Asia. The above points require further linguistic research.[12]

Moreover, the tendency of agglutination in Tibetan towards the morphological change accommodates the Sanskritic inflexions of *subanta, tinganta, pratyaya* and *upasarga.* The Tibetan texts from the Indian languages, Pali and Apabhramsha follow the above orthodoxy in order to maintain uniformity in translations (*sgyur yig*). No such methodical order could be innovated by the eminent translators like Kumarajiva, Fa-hsien, Hsuan Tsang for the linguistic bifurcation between Chinese and Tibetan in genesis.[13] Also, many loan words are floating in Tibetan as those had been accepted in the literary language (*gzhung yig*) and colloquial speech (*phal skad*). Even now, a sizeable number of Chinese phonemes have been adopted in the Modern Tibetan language used in the TAR (Tibet Autonomous Region).

The above points were further substantiated in the Tibetan grammatical texts namely Sumrtags (*Sum cu pa* and *Rtags 'jug pa*) accredited to Anu or Thon mi Sambhoṭa of the seventh cent. A. D. These texts are composed in verses with cryptic expressions. The former text has thirty verses as the title suggests. The latter text *Rtags 'jug pa* deals with characteristics of thirty letters and their grammatical applications in the language. Anu or Thon mi Sambhoṭa is said to have learnt Sanskrit grammar from an Indian grammarian Vidyākara-siṁha and he was asked by King *Srong btsan sgam po* (d. 650 A.D.)[14] to compose the grammatical texts for Tibetan. Subsequently his compositions were codified and preserved in the Tanjur (*bstan 'gyur*) collection.[15]

The aphoristic texts have several commentaries for elucidation of cryptic expressions with reference to the phonetics, morphology and syntax in an indigenous method.

Among the important commentaries some commentaries by the eminent scholars like *Dbyangs can dgan 'ba'i blo gros* (c. 15th cent A.D.).[16] Situ Panchen (18th cent. A.D.)[17], Lhag, sam (a follower of Situ, 17th cent A.D.), Dren dbang rtsis zur rgya mtsho (c. 16th cent A.D. of *Pa lung ka* monastery near Sera), *Dkon mchog chos grags* (17th cent), *Chos mdzad lo tsa ba* (18th cent A.D.), *Blo bzang Tshul khrims rgya mtsho* (19th cent. A.D.) deserve mention. The root treatises have been followed in both scriptural language *(chos skad)* as well as in literary works (*gzung yig*). A recent book on Tibetan Grammar by Nechog Gngul chu yab sras from Dharmasala in 1986 is the latest.

Outside Tibet, the grammatical analyses in commentary manner developed in Mongolia. *Tsan skya Khutuktu*[18] and Rol pa'i rdorje took efforts to prepare grammatical treatises. On the early Tibetan and Medieval Tibetan usages in the *gsungs bum* in seven volumes, in Tibet, the history of Tibetan changed through several epochs by separate councils of the academicians. The grammarians conducted discourses on the development of the Tibetan Language. Three important councils are generally enumerated in the growth of Tibetan.[19]

1. During the reign of *Khri srong lde' btsan* (8th cent)
2. At the lifetime of *Sa skya Pan chen* (13th cent)
3. By the initiative of Rgyal ba Nga ba (17th cent)

In China, several attempts in compilation of Tibetan words used in different context had been made; such as, Huo yuan chieh in his Hua i yi yu, in two volumes and the work *Ch'in ting hsi yu t'ung wen chi* (1766). *Bzod pa and Kun* dga'don grub translated in Mongolian a Tibetan dictionary, *Bod kyi skad las gsar rnying gi brda' bkod pa*[20] of ancient dictions.

It may not be out of place to mention that traditional commentaries lay emphasis on the formation of monosyllabic words and their uses with reference to the cases in respect of the noun, (*ming*). The adjectives (*yon tan*) are governed by the nouns. And the verbs (*bya ba*) have been broadly classified in three tenses, past (*'das pa*) present (*da lta ba*) and future (*ma 'ongs pa*) though a verb-root may be used as the noun or the adjective as required, depending on the conditionality or context. In that respect the particles (*tshig phrad*) play an important role in morphology and syntax. The Tibetan language therefore has less stress on the conjugation and the declension as those become inflexional in Sanskrit. The genesis of Tibetan is neither related to Sanskrit nor to Chinese.

In the European Languages

The westerners became curious of the Tibetans since the 14th century A. D. when the Franciscan missionaries like William of Rubruck had the occasion to witness a reincarnated boy of ten years old with yellow robes who was said to have triumphed in scriptural debate on Buddhism in China. William carried the six lettered prayer *OM MAṆI PADMĖ HŪṀ*. Subsequently, Marco Polo visited the Yuan court in China. He was wondered to notice that the Tibetan monks had been efficient in controlling the weather. John of Montecorvine also found one 'Red-hat' Tibetan priest, who might be a Sa skya teacher Ye shes rin chen in the Yuan court of China.

However, the first book of Tibetan text was composed by a Roman Missionary named *Alphabetinum Tebetinum* in the eighteenth century. No grammatical text was attempted by the missionaries in spite of their great zeal to master the language for rendering catholic service among the Asians. Frederic Christian Gotthelf Schröter compiled a dictionary of Bhotanta or Bhoutan language a prefactory note on Bhotanta language in 1826. Alexandar Csoma de Körös of

Hungary who had been in the western India at Pooh, Kanam had learnt Tibetan from Sangs rgyas phun tshogs and composed '*A Grammar of the Tibetan Language* in English'and that was published at Calcutta in 1834. A new epoch of the Tibetan language study began since then. He further ventured to compile a *Tibetan-English Dictionary.* He also edited and translated the *Mahāvyutpatti*, the Sanskrit-Tibetan bilingual lexicon, into English. His work was partially published by Sir Denison Ross, by Satish Chandra Vidyabhusana in two parts in 1910 and its remaining portion was published by Durga Charan Chatterjee in 1941 from the Asiatic Society of Bengal. Subsequently Ryoza-buro Sakaki made study on *Mahāvyutpatti* in 1916 and Kyoo Nishio prepared its Tibetan index (Kyoto 1936) Csoma's Tibetan grammar was distributed in the western method with separate sections, and Sarat Chandra Das appended Situ's commentary in his *Tibetan Grammar* (Darjeeling 1915). Rahul Sankrityayana made a daring task to prepare an indigenous Tibetan grammar in the model of Sanskrit grammar with *subanta, kāraka, vibhakti, samāsa, tinganta.*[21]

The works of the Hungarian scholar Csoma de Körös are regarded as the pioneer contributions by the westerners in the European languages. And, those could pave the path of further studies of Tibetan in Europe. Another grammar of the Tibetan language was attempted in Europe by Issac Jacob Schmidt (Schmidt, Jakov Ivanovich) entitled *Grammatika tibetskago iazyka* in Russian with its German translation *Grammatik der tibetischen Sprache* from St. Petersberg in 1839. After a couple of decades Philipe Edouard Foucaux published his study on Tibetan Grammatical critique in *Grammaire de la langue tibetaine* from Paris in 1858. Jacques Bacot studied the Thonmi's text with commentaries in 1928 and that was published from Paris in 1928 and his grammar of Tibetan in French appeared in 1948.

Following that, several researches of Heinrich August Jäschke, a Moravian missionary appeared on the Tibetan language and its critical studies came in the European journals on the morphological changes in the verb system and phonetics pubiished in the journal *Monatsberichte* (1860, 1865 & 1867). He also composed a Tibetan Grammar which became a handy companion of the non Tibetan learners in the nineteenth century. Its third edition with addenda by August Hermann Francke assisted by Walter Simon came out from Berlin in 1929. Herbert Bruce Hanna's *A Grammar of the Tibetan Language (literary and colloquial)*, Calcutta 1912 is an important work.

It may be added that Jäschke had pointed out the phonetic peculiarities of Tibetan pronunciation with reference to its dialects. The colloquial Tibetan (*phal skad*) differs from the literary language (*gzhung skad*). Graham Sandberg studied those peculiarities carefully and published *Handbook of the Colloquial Tibetan* from Calcutta 1894. Also Vincent Henderson's *Tibetan Manual*, Baptist Mission Press, Calcutta 1903 deserve mention. In our century the Tibetan language studies have developed in diverse dimensions in the European languages. Those may be broadly jotted down below.

Structural Linguistics: Morphology

Apart from the grammatical indigenous works, many linguists like Max Walleser studied on the structural pattern of Tibetan in his research articles on the subordinate clauses in Tibetan and on the Tibetan affirmative and the interrogative sentences in the *Indian Linguistics* (1935). Anton Schiefner initiated Tibetan studies on structural linguistics in his series of articles published in the *Bulletin de l'Academic des Sciences*, St. Petersberg since 1851. Hungarian scholars like Geza Uray published papers on the morphology in Tibetan in *Acta Academiea.* Hungarcaue (1953, 1954, 1958), Ray,

Andreu Miller's article on Morphologica Determined Allomorphos in Spoken Tibetan (*Language* 1954) became a scientific research in Tibetan linguistics. George N. Roerich studied on Tibetan dialects of Lahul (*Urusvati Journal 1933*).

Phonetic Studies

August Hermann Francke's article *Kleine Beiträge zur Phonetik and Grammatik des Tibetischen* (1903) was followed with an article addenda in *Toung pao* (1916), on the Tibetan phonology by Berthhold Laufer. J. H. Edgar further took care of the tonal system in Tibetan in *Williams Charles Border Research Society Journal* (1932). A. H. Francke dealt with the Tibetan pronunciation system in the early twentieth century in his learned article entitled 'Das tibetische Pronominal' system. Also, Ray Andrew Miller's learned paper 'the phonemes of Tibetan U-Tsang dialect' in *Journal of the Asiatic Society (Letters)* in 1951 focused a new light prior to George N. Roerich's *Textbook on Colloquial Tibetan U-Tsang dialect* (Calcutta, 1954) in collaboration with Lobsang phun tshogs.

Comparative Linguistics

In comparison with Indo-Chinese the causative denominative structures and those in Tibetan, August Conrady published an article from Leipzig (1896) and the said paper was reviewed in *T'oung Pao* (1897) by E. Von Zach. Bernhard Karlgren who made a comparative estimate of Chinese and Tibetan in T'oung pao (1931).

Again, Sten Konow published his comparative study on the spoken Languages between Assam Valley and Tibet in the *Journal of the Royal Asiatic Society* (1902).

Also Li Fang Kuei suggested a programme for the methodology of Sino-Tibetan linguistics in *Sinological*

Studies (1951). Wang Ching-ju's article on '*A comparative study of numerals and the personal pronouns in Chinese, Tai, Burmese and Tibetan* was published in Academica Sinica (1931) in Chinese.

Tibetan Orthography

By the last quarter of the nineteenth century many western linguistics explored various aspects of Tibetan as mentioned above. F. B. Shawe published his study paper in the *Journal of the Asiatic Society of Bengal* (1894) 'on the relationship between Tibetan Orthography and the original pronunciation of the language'. Geza Urai also studied on some knotty problems in Tibetan letters like 'ba'and 'wa', in 'A Tibetan Dimunitive Suffix' and 'Duplication Gemination and triplication' in *Acta Academiac Hungaraque* (1953, 1954, 1955 respectively). Recent studies on Tibetan language in Republic of China deserve mention, such as, Notes on the comparative study of Synonym compounds in Chinese and Tibetan by the author may be added here. For comparative grammar of Sanskrit and Tibetan, M.M. Vidhusekhara Bhattacharya Sastri elaborately dealt in his *Bhotaprakasha*, Calcutta University 1939. Max Wellesar also studied in this field as his work *Zur Aussprache des Sanskrit and Tibetischen* came in light from Heidelberg 1936. In this connection E. Obermiller published Indices Verborum to the *Nyaya bindu* (2 parts) in *Bibliotheca Buddhica* XXV. Satish Chandra Vidyabhusana took efforts in Sanskrit Tibetan bilingual index works of *Sragdhara Stotra (1908), Mahavyutpatti* (1913), *Nyayabindu* (1917).

Prospective Scope

Since 1959 the Tibetan language studies have bifurcated in two channels. (i) Led by the traditional Tibetan academicians who have been outside their homeland.

(ii) Conducted by the progressive academicians belonging to the TAR (Tibet Autonomous Region) of China and the Tibetan knowing scholars of China. As the result of such state of affairs, the linguistic studies in Tibetan have availed a new focus with the contemporary relevance in the both channels. Several studies on the grammatical texts in Sanskrit and Tibetan have come out in the last four decades by the Tibetan speaking academicians who are well versed in Sanskrit and Pali. Also some Sanskrit knowing scholars, who are conversant in Tibetan have undertaken the study of Tibetan Grammar from angle of the Sanskrit Grammar.

On the other hand several research works on Tibetan linguistics and dialects have already been published from China. The recent Seminar on Tibetan Language study in Beijing shows a new approach. Also, among the westerners, sustained efforts continue to study the Tibetan grammar, phonetics, morphology which are relative points with reference to the scientific methodology of Linguistics.

Notes

1. Tibet has ethnic diversity since the beginning of her history. Sum pa mkhan po (1704-1788 A.D.) refers to a few legendary ethnic groups like Mu, Se, ldong, Stong gra, Bru, (Dpag bsam ljon bzang, p148, Calcutta 1902); Gelek. The Tibetan plateau—one of the Homes of Early Man, *Anthropology of Tibet and the Himalayas* pp. 112f.
2. Haarh Erik, *The Yar lung Dynasty*, pp. 18f.
3. Petech Lussanio, *A Study of the History of Ladakh*, p. 32.
4. Grierson; *Linguistic Survey of India*, 1934, Vol III. 3.
5. Laufer, Berthold: *The Loan words in Tibetan*, Toung pao, 1916 pp. 403-552.
6. *T'ang shu*, chuan (chapter 3 folio 12).
7. Norbu Namkhai, *The Necklace of gzi, A Cultural History of Tibet*, Dharamsala, pp 42ff.

8. *Ibid.*, pp 63f; Haarth E.: *The Zhang Zhung Language*, Introduction.
9. Published from Delhi, by the Bon Foundation of India, Occhaghat.
10. Thomas: *The Tibetan Documents from Chinese Turkestan*, p. 6ff.
11. Karlgren, Bernhard: *Chinese and Tibetan*, p. 14 f.; also Grierson, *Linguistic Survey of India*, Vol III, pf. 3, p. 8 f.
12. *Encyclopaedia Britanica* (macropadia ed.) see the Korean and Japanese languages.
13. Nanjio, Bunyiu: *A Catalogue of the Chinese Translation of the Buddhist Tripitaka.* Appendix ii, 59, ii, 45, 159; ii, 133.
14. *Bu ston Rin chen grub kyis chos 'byung* (Eng transl. by Obermiller) pp. 36f.
15. *Tohku Imperial University Catalogue*, Tokyo, Japan 1935.
16. *Rtags 'jug dgongs 'grel rab gsal snang ba zhes bya ba.*
17. *Situ'i gsung 'bum* refers to *Lung stong sum cu pa'i 'grel ba.* Vol. V. (LIWA collection). Sarat Chandra Das in his Tibetan Grammar appended the text.
18. Lokesh Chandra, *Satapitaka.* Materials of the Tibetan Literature.
19. Dawa Norbu: Indo-Tibetan Cultural Relations through the ages, *Bulletin of Tibet House,* 1998.
20. Tibetan language studies are of three division;
    (a) grammatical texts *(sum rtags)*, (b) orthography *(dag yig)*
    (c) lexicon (*tshig brjod).*
21. *Sgra la 'jug pa,* Calcutta, Mahabodhi Society of India, 1916.

Select Bibliography

*Tibetan and Chinese (*arranged in Tibetan alphabetical order)

Ka dpe bshad by Rin chen don grub

Skad bzhi shan sbyor ba'i me long

Sgra la 'jug pa ed. Rahul Sankrityan, Culcutta, 1916.

Sgra'i bstan bcos (bstan 'gyur sna tshogs, Toh. 4351)

Sgra sbyor bam po gnyis pa (bstan 'gyur sna tshogs, Toh. 4347)

Ch'in ting hsi yu t'ung wen chi, 8 volumes in Chinese; (3111 Geographical names of Central and Western Asia) 1766.

Rtag 'jug snying pa'i gsal bo me long (Appended to Sgra la 'jug pa ed. by Rahul Sankrityayan, Calcutta, Mahabodhi Society, 1916.

Rtag 'jug legs bshad

Rtag 'jug pa'i dka' gnad gsal·ba'i me long by Dbyangs can grub pa'i rdo rje.

T'ang shu (Chinese)

Rnams dbye brgyad dang bya byed la sogs khyad par mdo tsam brjod pa by Dbyangs can Dga' ba'i blo gros.

Dag yig mkhas pa'i 'byung gnas (Tibetan-Mongolian Dictionary *arqu-yin orun neretu toglagagsan dag yig* completed 1742) ascribed to Rol pa'i rdo rje.

Brda dag min tshig sgal ba by Dge bshes tshos grags, Lhasa, 1950, 2 Vols.

Bod rgya tshing mdzod chen mo (3 vols) Beijing 1985.

Ming gi rgya mtsho (Tibeto-Mongolian lexicon) by Kun dga' rgya mtsho, 1718.

Bye brag tu rtogs par byed pa (bstan 'gyur 'gyur toh. 4346) (Maha-vyutpatti).

Yul gangs tshan pa'i brda yang dag par sbyor ba'i bstan bcos kyi bye brog sum cu pa dang rtags kyi 'jug pa'i gzhung gi rnam par bshad pa (printed by Sarat Chandra Das, Tibetan Grammar, Darjeeling, 1915).

Lung du ston pa'i rtsa ba sum cu pa zhes bya ba (bstan 'gyur Toh. 4348).

Lung du ston pa rtags kyi 'jug pa zhes bya ba (bstan 'gyur Toh. 4349).

Sum rtags kyi ngo mtshar 'phrul gyi lde mig by Bstan 'dzin rin po che

Sum cu pa'i legs bshad ljon dbang by Dbangs can grub pa'i rdo rje.

Hua i yu yu (c bynese) by Huo yuan chich, written by 1389 in 24 volumes arranged according to the subject vols. 4 and 11 discuss Tibetan (Si-fan) vocabularies.

Works in other languages (upto 1899 A.D.)

1764 Alphabetinum Tibetanium, Roma.

1826 Schroeter, Frederic Christian Gotthelf: *A Dictionary of Bhotanta or Bhoutan Language,* Serampore.

1834 Csoma de Körös: *A Grammar of the Tibetan Language,* Calcutta.

— — *Essay towards a Dictionary, Tibetan and English* (prepared with the assistance of Bande Sangs rgyas phun tshogs) Calcutta.

1839 Schmidt, Jakov Jvanovich: *Grammatika tibetokugo iajyka,* St. Petersberg.

1841 Tibetisch-Deutsches Worterbuch nebst deutschem Wortregister.

1851 Schiefner (Franz) Anton (von) Tibetische Studien *Bulletin Academia Science,* St. Petersberg.

1863 Schlagintweit, Hermann de (ed.): Glossary of Tibetan Geographical Terms. *Journal of Royal Asiatic Society,* London.

1858 Foucaux, Phillipe Edouard: *Grammaire de la langue tibetaine,* Paris.

1871-1876 Jäschke, Heinrich August: *Handworterbuch der tibetischen Sprache,* Gnadan (See 1954 Mish J.L.)

1877-1880 Szechenyi Bela, Grof. Szechenyi, Bela Kele a zsiai utjanak eradmeyli, *Osszchasonlito szotar,* Budapest.

1881 *A Tibetan-English Dictionary,* London.

1891 Pongrades, Sandor: *Tibet-magyar nyeletanulmiyak,* Budapest.

1898-99 Laufer, Berthold: *Uber das 'vazur'. ein Beitrag zur phonetik der tibetischen & sprache.*

1899 Desgoding, Auguste: *Essai de grammire thibetaine pour le langaga parle,* Hongkong; *Dictionaire Thibetaine-Latin* Francise per les Missionnaires catholiques du Thibet, Hongkong.

Buddhism in Tibet: An Overview 3

Pranabananda Jash

The religious history of Tibet from its earliest times enveloped with mystic ideas and esoteric environment. But in the subsequent period profoundly Buddhist in all aspects of its social, cultural and religious life, it was until 1959, dominated by the monastic hierarchy.

The impact and influence of Buddhism on Tibet since its introduction in the seventh century A. D. has been very deep and significant for the development in almost every facet of the Tibetan history. According to the traditional account, Buddhism was introduced into Tibet during the life time of Srong btsan Sgam po, who died in 649 A. D. [1] But before the advent of Buddhism in the land of snow, the Bon (a type of animistic religion) prevailed which has later on left its traces on the later Buddhist development. [2] It is stated that the King of Tibet "who was the maker of the Tibetan nation........ married a Nepalese princess about the year A. D. 630; the young bride brought with her, her gods and priests; she was given a place in the Tibetan pantheon as an incarnation of the goddess Tara". [3] The same king married a daughter of the T'ang emperor T'ai Tsong, and she, likewise a Buddhist, was deified in the same way.

The geographical factor made this tiny land to achieve its historical and cultural aspirations from time to time. Lying on one of the highways from India to China, through Nepal,

Tibet was thus naturally and from the beginning open to Indian and to Chinese influences, and these are distinctly recognizable in religion—the history of Buddhism in Tibet, in Tibetan art, with the development of the Tibetan painted scroll; in architecture with the design of temples, monasteries, stupas, and in politics, with the institution of the Dalai Lama; in social structure, with a large segment of the male population becoming celibate monks; in language, with the creation of the Tibetan script for the purpose of translating Buddhist scriptures, and in literature, with the composition of thousands of Buddhist texts in a vast variety of genres.

Thus Buddhist thought, practice and institutions were imported into Tibet from India sometime in the mid seventh century A. D, developed rapidly by contacts with influential Buddhist figures of Kashmir and northern India. Although Tibetan Buddhist thought mainly inherits from India, there have also been important influences from China and Central Asia.

According to Tucci "The Buddhism entering Tibet came not only from India (by which is to be understood not only India proper but also its border regions Nepal and Kashmir) but also from present-day Afghanistan and Gilgit, from the cities along the caravan routes of Central Asia (then known as the Silk Routes), and from China. Buddhism has never refused to accept, rework and transform the ideas of other peoples. In the territories bordering on Tibet there existed numerous religious forms in a picturesque juxtaposition which favoured exchange and reciprocal borrowings. The Chinese translators of Nestorian and Manichaean texts borrowed technical expressions from Taoist and Buddhist terminology, and indeed they borrowed more than just terminology. Vajrayāna (gnostic) Buddhism developed hand in hand with Śaivism. It is probable that in these ways, through the meditation of Buddhists influence by other streams of thought or for that matter directly, ideas foreign to Buddhism could be introduced within it, and gradually be merged into a developing doctrinal structure".[4] Tibetan Buddhism is one of the major forms of Buddhism in this subcontinent, with its influence extending far beyond the geographical jurisdictions of Tibet, to the Kalmyk region of Russia near the Caspian Sea in the west, to Siberia in the north, to Mongolia, China and Manchuria in the east, and to Nepal in the south. This religious tradition is properly referred to as Tibetan Buddhism, rather than Lamaism, a term that mistakenly suggests that the religion of Tibet is not Buddhism. Giuseppe Tucci long ago observed that "Lamaism introduced here (Nepal) the habits of Tibet; but met here with other customs which enjoyed, in conformity with the practices formerly observed in Tibet by some Bon-Po, that the corpse should be cast in the rivers. And so the white scarf, still used in the funeral rites of some Bon-Po tribes on the boundaries of China, is the emblem of the rope which, in the original shaman form, joined, like a bridge, the earth to the sky and on which the deceased walked up. The old beliefs have not been fully abandoned: a compromised has been reached, and instead of casting the corpse into the river his image is thrown in it".[5] Bon has still retained its own identity to this day. In addition, there remains a vast area of rites and beliefs that are neither specifically Buddhist nor Bon but may be designated "Popular religion" or "the religion without a name". G. Tucci points out that "In any case Buddhism must have already, from its first entry into Tibet, undergone much modification and weakening. It cannot be denied that the local cults and beliefs persisted to a large degree, and that there were powerful centres of Bon resistance throughout the country".[6] In fact, the impact of Buddhism on this creed was so strong that the Bon came to have even a Bon Sans-rgyas or Bon Buddha and like the Dkon-mchog gsum—the *Buddha*, *Dharma* and *Sangha* of

Buddhism, the Bon developed their own Yung-drum gsum, the three svastikas. The Bon architecture, iconography and sacred furnishings are much common with those of Tibetan Buddhism. And just as Buddhism transformed the Bon religion, the latter in turn infected Buddhism itself for its existence. We see a whole mass of Du, and Nyan, Sadhak, thab-bha, pho-bha, i. e., the black demons, the orgies, the serpent spirits, the earth gods, the tutelary gods, creeping into the Buddhist pantheon on the Tibetan soil.

With the introduction of Buddhism in Tibet the religious scenario took a new form which was the outcome of an admixture between the Bon and the newly advent Buddhism. Buddhism is traditionally demarcated in terms of two distinct periods—the earlier and the later dissemination of the doctrines. The former started in the second half of the eighth century A. D. and interested the first translation of Buddhist texts from Sanskrit into Tibetan, the establishment of Buddhist monasteries and the patronage of Buddhism by the royal and the noble families. It ended with the suppression of Buddhism by king Lang Darma in 836 A. D.

The second Buddhist wave in Tibet began over a century later, i. e. in the later half of the tenth century A. D. It was marked by the translation of many Buddhist texts, exchange of Tibetan and Indian Buddhist monks and teachers, and the lineages of teaching established between India and Tibet ultimately gave rise to the major sects of Tibetan Buddhism.

Whatever may be the date of antiquity of Buddhism in Tibet, there is hardly any doubt that sustained Tibetan exposure to Buddhist thought and practice began at the end of the eighth century A. D., during the reign of King Trisong Detsen, when Śāntarakshita the reputed Indian Paṇḍita, was invited to Lhasa, the then Tibetan capital. [7] The Buddhist teachings preached by Śāntarakshita was not acceptable to all, and thus a section of the Tibetan people blamed him for a series of natural disasters on the introduction of the foreign faith. The Indian Paṇḍita was forced to retreat to Nepal, but before doing so, he advised the king to invite the Tantrika master Padmasambhava to Tibet. The king agreed, and according to the chronicles written several centuries later, Padmasambhava converted the demons of Tibet to the Buddhist fold, enlisting their promise to always protect the new faith. After sometimes, Śāntarakshita returned to Tibet, where he joined with Padmasambhava and the king to establish the first Buddhist monastery at Tibet in 779 A. D. Von, where several Tibetans were ordained as the first Buddhist monks, "after the foundation of Bsam-yas and the official recognition of Buddhism"[8] Padmasambhava remained a strong mythic presence for Tibetan Buddhism, Śāntarakshita and Padmasambhava were well versed in both Buddhist doctrine and Tantrik form of Buddhism. Through the Tibetan Buddhist tradition these two teachers played important role with the assertions of the various philosophical schools, Buddhist and non-Buddhist and also employed their expertise in ritual and in meditation for showing hidden powers. This practice continued during the time of Dharmasvamin.

But a tussle of doctrinal controversy erupted in Tibet when the Chinese Buddhist monks of the Ch'an(zen) school led by one Mo-ho-yen visited the Buddhist monastery at Samye in Tibet.[9] Tradition avers that Śāntarakshita professed of dangers from the Chinese position and left instructions in his will that his student Kamalaśīla be called from India to counter the Chinese view. The reason for conflict was over the question of the nature of enlightenment. The Indians held that enlightenment takes place as the culmination of a gradual process of purification, the result of combining virtuous action, meditative serenity and philosophical insight. The Chinese, on the contrary, believed that enlightenment was the intrinsic nature of the mind rather than the goal of a protracted path, such that one need simply to recognize the presence of this innate nature of enlightenment by entering a state of awareness beyond distinctions; all other practices are superfluous. According to both Chinese and Tibetan records, a debate was held between Kamalaśīla and Mo-ho-yen at Samye in 797 A.D. with king Trisong Detsen himself serving as judge. The Tibetan accounts (contradicted by the Chinese accounts) mention that Kamalaśīla defeated Mo-ho-yen, and thus he with his party left Tibet. The king then ordered that the Madhyamika school of Buddhist Philosophy (to which Śāntarakshita and Padmasambhava belonged) would be followed in Tibet.

A large number of Tibetan monks and scholars visited India, studied at Nalanda or Vikramasila and went back to their country to preach the fruits of their study. Chaglo-tsa-ba-Chos rje-dpal seems to be the only one among them who left notes about the account of India, her people, customs and institutions. [10] During the pre-Buddhist policy of the Malla kings several youths went to Kashmir to study Buddhist teachings. One of these youths was later to become eminent under the name of Rin chen bzang Po (958-1055 A.D). G. Tucci has pointed out that "Kashmir was an appropriate place not only because of its nearness, but also because the last splendour of the Buddhist schools then held away there, and famous religious teachers preserved both the speculative and logical tradition, and the practice of the Tantra and ritual. At the end of their education, the youths returned from Kashmir to their homeland, along with teachers and also some artists, and they began to propagandize their faith over a wide region under the protection of the court". [11]

In fact, Buddhism expanded through west Tibet and a galaxy of Buddhist scholars from India were invited to Tibet. It is generally believed that "after the death of K'ri sron lde btsan there was a strong revival of Indian Buddhism, caused not only by the direct instigation of court, anxious to prevent any further Chinese influence, but also by the growing prestige of the Indian and the coming of Indian ācāryas in greater number than before. Then Jñānamitra, Jñānendrabodhi, Śailendra, Dānaśīla, Bodhimitra, Ratnarakshita, Dharmatāśīla, Jñānasena, Jayarakshita, Mañjuśrīvarman, Ratnendrarakshita, etc. representing the new trend of Buddhism based on a careful study not only of the Law but also of Vyākaraṇa and eager to find a strict correspondence between Sanskrit and Tibetan undertook a great work of translation and revision. In this period, which, if we accept the date contained in the SGra abyer covers the reign of K'ri Ide sren btsen, the real consolidation of Indian Buddhism took place.[12] Specific conclusion on this point is not beyond doubt; but it is significant that from this point Tibet largely sought its Buddhism from India; and no school of Chinese Buddhism had any further influence in Tibet.

With the patronage of the Tibetan kings Buddhism flourished unprecedently. But the translation of Indian Buddhist literature—the *Sūtras, Śāstras* and *Tantras,* from Sanskrit into Tibetan was interrupted by the suppressions of Buddhist monastic institutions in 838 A. D. The Tibetan monarchy ended shortly thereafter with the assassination of king who had ordered the closing of the Buddhist monasteries. Internal turmoil and tussle for royal authority in political scenario checked the smooth progress and development of Buddhism for the time being. The status of Buddhist thought and practice during the next century and a half remains only vaguely understood by that scholars.

Thus Buddhism with its zeal and vigour again appeared in the eleventh-twelfth centuries A. D. when Tibetan monks and scholars came to India where they studied with Indian Buddhist teachers in Bihar, Bengal and Kashmir, and many of the sects of Tibetan Buddhism trace their lineages back to these encounters. It may be mentioned in this connection, for example, that the Kagyuhpa sect derives its lineage from the visits to India by Marpa the translator (1012-1099 A.D.), where he studied under several Tantrik teachers of the contemporary period, including Naropa and Maitripa. The Sakyapa sect looks back to another translator, Drok mi (993-1050 A.D.) who studied in India under disciples of the Tantrik teacher Virupa. It was the Sakyapa scholar Buton Rinchen Drub (1290-1364 A.D.) who systematised the various collections of Indian Buddhist texts circulating in Tibet into the well-known Kanjur (translation of the word of the Buddha), and the Tanjur (translation of the Śāstras). The Indian scholar to visit Tibet during the second dissemination was the famous Atisa (982-1054 A.D.) whose followers became the Kadampa sect, regarded as a forerunner of the Gelugpa. It is observed that "His (Atisa's) work had included not only the diffusion of the doctrine which had already been codified, but in particular a new emphasis on the cult of the goddess Tara, to whom he was especially devoted. He wrote concise texts to serve as introductions to leading on to a more profound study of the Buddhist doctrine of salvation. [13] On the basis of the account of Dharmasvamin (Biography of Dharmasvamin), it is stated that "Indian Buddhism had naturally exercised considerable influence over the Tibetan Buddhism in the literary and philosophical spheres. The practice of Tantrika processes and mystic maṇḍalas, the worship of deities like Aparajita, Khasarpana, Avalokiteśvara, Remata and Blue Achala and the study of Pāramitā works like *Ashtasahasrikās* and *Pañchaviṁśati-sahasrikās* had become very popular". [14] The work of Dharmasvamin also shows "that architecture also did not remain uninfluenced. It points out how the court-yard of the Vajrāsana temple had gates to the east, north and west but none to the south, and observes that Tibetan temples and monastic courtyards followed the example did not provide for any gate to the south".[15]

It is to be noted in this connection that during the Mongol Yuan dynasty (1260-1368 A.D.), Tibetan Buddhism played an important role at the court of Kublai Khan, where the emperor's Buddhist preceptor was the famous monk Pakpa (1280 A. D. ?) of the Sakyapa sect. Imperial titles were also bestowed on monks of the Kagyupa sect. Chinese emperors in the Ming dynasty (1368-1644 A. D.) continued to confer gifts and titles on Lamas of the Kagyupa, Sakyapa and Gelugpa sects. During the Qing (1644-1912 A. D.), however, especially from the time of the Kangxi emperor (r. 1661-1722 A. D), imperial favour was directed primarily toward the Gelugpas. Under the Qianlong emperor (r. 1736-1795 A. D.), for example, the entire Tibetan Kanjur was translated into Manchu under the direction of the Gelugpa hierarch Jangkya Hutuktu Rolpay Dorje (1717-1786 A.D.).

The origin of the Gelugpas is said to have inherited from the tradition of Atisa who arrived in Tibet in 1042 A. D. While dealing with the objective of his teaching, Tucci has pointed out: "The teaching aimed in the first place at the purification of mind (blo sbyong), at the realization of the ethical and esoteric principles of Buddhism. Much less time was devoted to Buddhism's highly-developed theoretical side. Essentially this instruction was limited to leading the disciple to a better understanding of his own mind and to the achievement of insight into 'Void-ness'as the limiting state of things (mthar-thug), together with compassion. The thought of enlightenment from the point of view of ultimate reality is equated with 'Voidness', while compassion results from the same thought when considered from the standpoint of conventional truth. 'Voidness' is the 'body of essence', compassion the 'body of form'.[16]

Tsong Khapa (1357-1419 A. D.) is one of the most

eminent figures of this sect. His contribution to the development can not be denied. He founded the monastery of Ganden (named after the Buddhist heaven Tushita) outside of Lhasa in 1409, A. D. and his followers were originally known as the Gandenpas. This eventually evolved to Gelug, 'the system of virtue'. The Gelugpas established large monastic organisations, like universities, institutions, etc. throughout Tibet and Mongolia, one of which, Drepung, was the largest Buddhist monastery in the world, with over 13000 monks in 1959.

The main trait of Tsong Khapa's work is the pursuit of consistency among apparently disparate or contradictory elements within Buddhist doctrine. He sought to demonstrate a harmony between sūtra and tantra, between reasoned analysis and contemplative experience, between conventional truth and ultimate truth. He claimed that it could be logically established that there is no contradiction between the validity of worldly categories (such as cause and effect, virtue and non-virtue), on the other hand, and the fact that those categories were empty, that is, ultimately lacking in any kind of intrinsic or independent nature, on the other. He also argued that the logical and systematic analysis of the constituents of experience is essential for the attainment of enlightenment. In this less technical works, he said that all of Buddhist practice could be encompassed under the categories of renunciation the compassionate aspiration to liberate all beings from suffering and the understanding that all phenomena are devoid of substantial or independent existence. He left a massive corpus of writings on a wide variety of topics, his most famous works being two compendia of practice, one detailing the exoteric path of enlightenment, the Great Exposition of the stages of the path to Enlightenment (Lam rim chen mo), and the other detailing the esoteric or tantric path, the Great Exposition of the stages of Mantra (Ngags rim Chen mo).

After his death, Tsong Khapa was deified by his followers. With the political ascendancy of the Gelug under the Fifth Dalai Lama, the exaltation of his legacy became more widely spread. Just as Padmasambhava is spoken of simply as the 'precious guru', Tibetans often refer to Tsong Khapa as the 'precious lord'.

Tibetans share with all Buddhists a belief in a cycle of beginningless rebirth called *Samsāra*, where beings are reborn according to the law of *karma.* In brief, virtuous actions, such as charity and preserving life result in happiness in the future, while non-virtuous deeds of body (like murder), speech (i. e. lying), and mind (i. e. wishing others ill) result in suffering. The effects of these deeds not only determine where one will be reborn after death. There are six possible places of rebirth viz., the realms of gods, demigods, humans, animals, hungry ghosts, and hell beings. The state beyond suffering is called *nirvāna.* In the early Buddhist tradition, the goal seems to have been for each person to strike for his or her own liberation from rebirth. With the rise of the Mahāyāna, the goal was expanded to include the liberation of all beings.

Although the various sects of Tibetan Buddhism derive their monastic regulations from the Indian school known pejoratively as the Hīnayāna (lesser vehicle), all schools of Tibetan Buddhism identify themselves as proponents of the Mahāyāna (great vehicle), both in their practice and in their philosophy. Perhaps the most famous feature of the Mahāyāna is its emphasis on the Bodhisattva, a person who makes the compassionate vow to become a Buddha in order to lead all beings in the universe out of suffering and to the bliss of enlightenment. The term *bodhisattva* was rendered into Tibetan as "one who is heroic in his or her aspiration to enlightenment".

Bodhisattvas having emanated from higher state, or having risen from the imperfect state of ordinary men to that of Arhat, are fully qualified to become Buddhas. The Boddhisattvas choose not 'to disappear like a flame freed from name and form'. They sacrificed for the liberation in the midst of suffering humanity sharing their experiences as incarnations and lifting them from their lot—*Karman*, *Karuṇā* or compassion gains supremacy over self-centred individual *moksha* or release. In fact, the core of the entire Tibetan attitude to life, in conformity with this ideal, is *Karuṇā*, their spiritual leader, the Dalai Lama, is *Karuṇā's* incarnation par excellence. He dominates by the power of love through the conquest of the heart. Another important incarnation is Pānchen Lama representing flod-dpag-med or Amitabha—Infinite light—the Dhyānī-Buddha of the existing *kalpa*. Moreover, there are several incarnate Lamas called *tulkus* who are believed to be incarnations of accomplished Indian, Tibetan or Mongolian saints. The concept of Lama in Tibetan Buddhism occupies a significant role in the spiritual tradition of the order of monks.

The Bodhisattva who is said to be the physical manifestation of all the compassion of all the Buddhas in the universe, Avalokiteśvara, is the particular object of such reverence in Tibet, where it is believed that this Bodhisattva-form takes successive human births as the Dalai Lama. Avalokiteśvara is invoked by the famous mantra: *Om mani Padme Hum* [O you who hold the jewelled (rosary) and the lotus have mercy on us]. The Avalokiteśvara-form of Bodhisattva is very popular and is also depicted in a wide variety of forms in Tibetan art-two of the most frequent being with one head and four arms; and the other with eleven heads and a thousand arms. The multiple arms are said to represent the Bodhisattva's extraordinary ability to come to the aid of suffering sentient beings.

In fact, the main traits of Tibetan Buddhism are to be found after Atisa who introduced the later form of Mahāyāna Buddhism, viz., Vajrayāna, Mantrayāna, Kālachakrayāna, and other practices. Thus, the later Buddhist practices in Tibet witnessed the assimilation of the most important development of late Indian Tantrik Buddhism. This practice was considered an esoteric approach to the Mahāyāna path whereby time required to achieve Buddhahood could be shortened from the standard length of three periods of countless as one to as little as three years and three months. The Tantrik scriptures are eloquent enough to instruct the technique for effecting such an extraordinary power through an elaborate system of rites, rituals, meditation, etc. These are all very significant feature and symbolic too.

The representations of the erotic and wrathful motifs, where male and female are depicted in sexual union and bullheaded deities, adorned with garlands of human heads, brandish cleavers and skull cups, are the very common elements of Tantrik Buddhism in Tibet. It is believed that *prajñā* (wisdom) and *karuṇā* (compassion) are the essential components of the Bodhisattva's path to Buddhahood. Wisdom (*prajñā*) especially the perfection of wisdom, is identified with the female. In Tantra, the symbolism is revealed in more explicitly sexual terms, with wisdom as female and method male, their union being essential to the achievement of enlightenment. Buddhist Tantra is said to be the 'Diamond Vehicle'(Vajrayāna) because wisdom and method are joined in an adamantine and indivisible union, bestowing Buddhahood quickly. This is the general accept meaning of the depiction of sexual union.

Similarly, the wrathful depiction of the deities in the Tibetan Buddhist pantheon, also bears adequate significance. It may be the continuation of Tibetan Shamanic origin who were added to Indian Buddhism after its arrival in Tibet. These wrathful deities are described vividly in the Buddhist Tantras. According to the Tantrik scriptures some of these deities are Buddhas and Bodhisattvas in their wrathful aspects the most famous being *Yamantaka*, the wrathful manifestation of the Bodhisattva of wisdom, *Mañjuśrī*. He is popular and favourite tutelary deity of the Gelugpa sect. Some of these wrathful deities have the task of projecting the *dharma* or to protect from some malignant forces and untoward exigencies as the manifestation of deity or a particular aspect of a deity.

In order to appease the deities the Tibetan Buddhist makes daily practices of worship to a Buddha, a Bodhisattava, or a particular deity, and an image of that deity was therefore employed for that purpose. As mentioned earlier the representation of wrathful deities were believed to offer protection to their owners; various deities whose powers were of the more mundane variety, such as, the god of wealth, were depicted and venerated for the boons they could bestow. As per the Tibetan practices images were not considered merely symbolic representations, because each statue and *thangka* after its completion would be consecrated, in the belief that the principle of enlightenment called the *Dharmakāya* (Truth Body of the Buddha) would come to inhabit the image. In the case of statues, the consecration ceremony required that the inside of a hollow image be filled with scrolls of *mantras* and various sacred substances and then sealed. It is believed that it will be considered most inauspicious if anyone opens the bottoms of such statues and empty out their contents.

It is, however, to be noted that the Pandits or monks whose lives were spent largely in the performance of Tantrika ritual or in various forms of meditation, in an effort to manifest a fantastic world of benign and malevolent forces, propitiating deities and repelling demons, by performing Tantrika instructions or techniques for drawing *maṇḍalas*, making rain, stopping diseases like smallpox, snake-bite, etc., and manufacturing magical pills.

In fact, the representation of different categories of Buddhas and Bodhisattvas is not without any philosophical significance. The self creative *Ādi-Buddha* creates by thought of the *Dhyānī-Buddhas* who live in perpetual *Nirvāna* with a *Dharma-kāya*, body of Truth-essence, not a Physical body. From the *Dharmakāya Buddhas* emanate the *Sambhogakāya Bodhisattvas* and from them in turn the *Nirmānakāya Mānushi Buddhas*. *Sambhoga* is experience of infinite happiness. In Buddhism, however, the term has been transformed from its ordinary meaning of carnal pleasure to spiritual beatitude. Whereas the *Dhyānī-Buddhas* live in meditation, the *Dhyānī Bodhisattvas* experience supreme happiness, not through the medium of senses, but in mind state. It is, however, believed that once in every *kalpa* (world cycle) they do assume *Nirmānakāya*, a mortal frame built of the elements, viz., earth, air, fire, etc. Gautama Buddha is regarded as the *Mānushi-Buddha* of the present, the fourth cycle, and *Avalokiteśvara*, it's *Dhyānī-Bodhisattva*, Creator. In the Tibetan tradition there are five *Dhyānī-Bodhisattvas* in the *Trikāya* system:

(i) Kun-tu-bzan-po (*Samanta Bhadra*)—the all benign;

(ii) Phyag-na-rdo rje (*Vajrapāṇi*)—the bearer of thunderbolt;

(iii) Phyag-na-rin-chen (*Ratnapāṇi*)—the jewel-bearer;

(iv) Spyan-ras-gzigs (*Avalokiteśvara*) of compassionate look; and

(v) Phyag-na-sna-tshoga-rdo-rje (*Viśvapāṇi*)—crossed thunderbolt bearers.

Several other Bodhisattvas, like Byams-Pa (*Maitreya*), Hjam-dpal (*Mañjuśrī*), Snam-snan *(Ākāśagarbha)*, Sahi-snin (*Kshitigarbha*), Hjig-rton (*Trailokya-Vijaya*), Sagrib-Pa-rnam-sel (*Sarva-nivarana-Vishkambhin*), etc. representing various aspects of divinity, such as, love, compassion, beatitude, strength, dominion, etc. are also prevalent. The witness of female Bodhisattvas are not unknown. Thus Dbyans-can-ma (*Sarasvatī*) associated with learning and fine arts; Nor-rgyun ma (*Vasudharā*) with abundance; Ses-rab-kyi pha-rottu-phyin-pra *(Prajñāpāramitā)* with transcendental wisdom and others are endowed with various powers and attributes.

In fact, there has been little development in the realm of philosophical ideas: the Tibetans have, on the whole, been content to play the role of exegetes, commentators, and compilers. However, the political domination that the monasteries gradually obtained was without precedent. An uniquely Tibetan feature of monastic rule was succession by incarnation-the head of an order, or of a monastery, being regarded as the re-incarnation of his predecessor. In other cases, a religious figure might be regarded in the person of the fifth Dalai Lama (1617-1682 A.D.) both ideas were combined. Each Dalai Lama[17] was already regarded, as the incarnation of his predecessor; the fifth, who established himself as head of the Tibetan state, also came to be regarded as the emanation or manifestation of the great *Bodhisattva Avalokiteśvara* (Tib. spyan-ras-gzigs), as have all subsequent Dalai Lamas down to the present, the fourteenth. [18]

Thus the choice of *Avalokiteśvara* was not made at random. As early as the twelfth or thirteenth century A.D., *Avaloketiśvara*, it is believed assumed the role of progenitor of the Tibetan people in order to realise that the teachings of the Buddha might flourish in Tibet in due course during the time of the great Tibetan king Sron-btsan-sgam-po (seventh century A.D.). Thus, *Avalokiteśvara* had established Buddhism—according to this retrospective view-in the land of snow. The Potala palace in Lhasa, the ancient capital, was built in its present form by the fifth Dalai Lama and made his residence; situated on a hill, it symbolically re-established the pre-Buddhist connection between the divine king and the sacred mountain. It thus shows that the incarnation of *Avalokiteśvara, i.e.* the Dalai Lama became the temporal authority over all sects beside being the spiritual authority over the Gelug-pa or the Yellow Hat sect. This is possibly one of the earliest references to the contribution of the Tibetan Buddhists in the realm of Buddhism.

Notes and References

1. Giuseppe Tucci, *The Religions of Tibet,* (translated from the German and Italian by Geoffrey Samuel) First paper-back printing, University of California Press, p. 1.

2. S. C. Das, A brief sketch of the Bon religions. . . . . *Journal Buddhist Text Society*, India, I, 1893, Haskin, pp. 116-17; cf. also A. K Coomaraswamy, *History of Indian and Indonesian Art,* 1965, New York, p. 146.

3. A. K. Coomaraswamy, *op. cit.*, p. 147.

4. G. Tucci, *op. cit.*, p. 15.

5. G. Tucci, *Preliminary Report on two Scientific Expedition in Nepal,* Rome, 1956, Serio Orientale Role, vol. x, pt. i. p. 27; *The Tibetan Book of the Dead,* Oxford University Press, 3rd edition, 1960 paperback.

6. G. Tucci, *The Religions of Tibet,* p. 15.

7. S. C. Das, Indian Pandits in Tibet, *Journal of Buddhist Texts Society of India.* I, 1893.

8. G. Tucci, *Minor Buddhist Texts,* Delhi, 1986, p. 336.

9. B. Lipton and N. Dorjee Rȧgnubas, *Treasures of Tibetan Art,* Oxford, 1996, p. 20.

10. *Biography of Dharmasvamin,* ed. G. Roerich, K. P. Jayaswal Institute, Patna, p. i.

11. G. Tucci, *The Religions of Tibet*, p. 21.

12. G. Tucci, *Minor Buddhist Texts,* Delhi, 1986, p. 360.

13. G. Tucci, *The Religions of Tibet*, p. 22; cf. also Aloka Chattopadhyaya, *Atisa and Tibet.* New Delhi, 1986.

14. *Biography of Dharmasvamin* (Chag lo-tsa-ba Chos-rje-dpal, a Tibetan monk pilgrim of the first half of the thirteenth century

A. D.), by Dr. G. Roerich, K. P. Jayaswal Institute, Patna, p. iii.

15. *Ibid.*, p. 73.

16. G. Tucci, *The Religions of Tibet*, p. 23.

17. The Dalai Lamas at a glance:

    I. Gedun Truppa—1391-1475 A. D.
    II. Gedun Gyatso—1475-1543 A. D.
    III. Sonam Gyatso—1543-1588 A. D.
    IV. Yonten Gyatso—1589-1617 A. D.
    V. Ngawang Lobzang Gyatso—1617-1682 A. D.
    VI. Tsangyang Gyatso—1683-1706 A. D.
    VII. Kezang Gyatso—1708-1757 A. D.
    VIII. Jampel Gyatso—1758-1805 A. D.
    IX. Luntok Gyatso—1806-1815 A. D.
    X. Tshultrim Gyatso—1816-1837 A. D.
    XI. Khedrup Gyatso—1838-1856 A. D.
    XII. Trinle Gyatso—1856-1875 A. D.
    XIII. Thupten Gyatso—1876-1933 A. D.
    XIV. Tenzin Gyatso—b. 1935-

18. *Encyclopedia of Religion*, ed. Mircea Eliade, Vol. 14, 1987, pp. 500ff.

Personal Observations on Tibetan Language and Literature

4

Lama Chimpa

Tibetan is a highly respected language that has been spread all over the world in the past four decades, along with the stream of Tibetan refugees and the increasing interest in the subject of Tibetology.

In India and the neighbouring Himalayan regions several lakhs of people speak Tibetan, including the Bhutanese, Ladakhis and Bhutias of Sikkim. In spite of the variation in dialect and their names, all of them speak Tibetan, and their written language is the same.

The differences in the Tibetan dialects are very large. Almost each and every township and district follows its own dialect. Therefore, sometimes two Tibetans from different regions face difficulties in communicating and understanding each other. But if they are to write their messages their communication will be easy. Unfortunately many of them are illiterate and such case, have to rely on sign language.

The written Tibetan is quite different from the spoken Tibetan. The forms of written Tibetan can never be changed. Its spelling is the life of the language. If the spelling of a term is incorrect, nobody will be able to relate to its meaning. For example: khepa; by writing it the way it is pronounced it cannot be understood literally. Does it mean "a profit maker"? In its transliteration mkas pa, however, there is no confusion in understanding its meaning as "a learned man". Thus, someone who knows the spoken language and may be even the Tibetan script, still may not be able to write a single word. As well as he will have difficulties in reading the written Tibetan. Even if someone would read out the text to him he will not understand. Thus he still would be considered illiterate.

Countless of Tibetan grammar books have been written over the centuries. Each of the grammarians tried to point out further details which would help in learning the language. But eventually all reach at the same point, as there is no scope in changing the spelling or the tenses of the age-old fixed rules of the Tibetan language.

There have been several foreign scholars among those Tibetan grammarians, most of them are very interested in the style and grammar of the language. That is perhaps why most of the foreign Tibetologists wrote Tibetan grammar books. All books explain the same rules in different ways. None of the scholars has attempted to simplify the language and to change its written form. Pandit Rahul Sankrityayana (1893-1963) was the only exception.

His unique style of Tibetan is reflected in his Sanskrit-Tibetan and Hindi-Tibetan dictionaries, published by the Sahitya Academy, New Delhi. As far as I know his theories were not widely welcomed. In fact, many people were heard saying that Rahulji was not very well-versed in written Tibetan and that therefore his Tibetan writings were erroneous.

Changing the model of a well-established language such as Tibetan is not to be taken lightly. Indian Tibetologists, such as Prof. Suniti Kumar Pathak, by translating some of Rabindranath Tagore's Bengali writings into Tibetan, following his own ways, have not received much of acceptance from Tibetan scholars. In the past, those scholars who tried to interfere with their traditional linguistic rules of literature, have not been received kindly by the Tibetan community.

An effective modification of a traditional language such as Tibetan would need a long struggle and a lot of scholarly and public debates. The issue has been frequently discussed among the Tibetan community themselves, as more and more Tibetans in exile lose touch with their indigenous literature. I feel, that if there is at all a change necessary in the written Tibetan, it would imply a nation-wide movement.

Such a movement has been observed in China where an entire nation had to be mobilised to simplify the old scripts. Thousand of school books and texts had to be rewritten, guidelines with the old and new scripts, both printed in large issues and distributed freely around the country. Newspapers and magazines had to be printed in the new scripts, as well as, orders issued to people and institutions to only use the simplified scripts. I believe the movement was only partially successful, resulting in scholars still preferring the old form of writing and the new generations not being able to read their classical literature.

A similar situation might occur if the beautiful Tibetan classical language is going to be revised. Then the future generations of Tibetans would not be able to read their classical literature which has been the life of the Tibetan culture and language. Because of all the dialects there seems to be no way to reform the spoken language in accordance with the written language and vice versa. Thus, the spoken and written Tibetan will have to remain apart for ever.

I remember the statement of an English grammarian: "Language is a living thing. It keeps on changing with the times". The grammar of a language cannot force the people to follow its rules, but the grammar has to follow the people. It shows the ways of how the people speak. For the Tibetans this case is different. The Tibetan grammar does not follow the people. It only follows the written form of classical Tibetan.

The wide differences between the spoken and written language may be creating problems among the Tibetans. For outside scholars who are basically concerned with the written language it hardly makes any difference. Tibetologists in their research should mainly focus on the various aspects of the classical Tibetan. A change in the written language, based on the spoken principles, would disturb them. For the non-Tibetan scholars Tibetan means the classical and modern written Tibetan. To them, spoken Tibetan is secondary.

One example is given here based on my study life in Mongolia: The entire Mongolian race, including Inner and Outer Mongols, and the Buryat and Shingjian Mongols, used to sutdy Tibetan on a large scale. Each year, thousands of Mongol students received admission in one of the large monasteries where the medium of education was Tibetan. I myself was one of them in the 1940s. After reviving the necessary knowledge of classical Tibetan, I studied Buddhist philosophy, all in Tibetan. Even then I never knew that there were Tibetan speaking people. I thought that Tibetan is only a medium of study. After completing my studies on philosophy I reached Tibet and was unable to say a single word in Tibetan. But there was no problem in pursuing higher studies as the medium was once again the classical Tibetan that I was familiar with.

About Tibetan Literature

The vast canon of Tibetan literature has its origin in the translation movements that took part during the first and second spread of Buddhism in Tibet (7th-12th century AD). The first Buddhist King Srong Tsan Gampo (srong btsan sgam po; died in 650) sent 17 students under the guidance of his minister Thomi Sambhota to India to learn Sanskrit. After having studied the year-long hardships he returned to Tibet. There Thomi framed the Tibetan characters and laid the base of Tibetan literature. It is said that he wrote eight grammar books which became the first Tibetan literature. Ever since thousands of great scholars have lived in Tibet and translated and created a huge corpus of beautiful literature. The works that were translated from Sanskrit were collected and compiled in two great canons, the Kanjur ('kha 'gyur) and Tanjur (bstan 'gyur). The Kanjur comprises the sayings of the Buddha in 108 volumes. The Tanjur is a collection of 225 volumes of works by Indian scholars. Of course, these are mostly Buddhist literature, but there are also a few non-Buddhist works included in the Tanjur, e.g. the *Meghaduta* and *Shakuntala* by Kalidas.

I also remember a beautiful work called *Dhatuparivartana Shastra* which is also included in the Tanjur. In this work Nalina teaches how one can turn base metal into gold. Chemical elements that are used in this process are listed in this book. It seemed to me like a work of modern science, mentioning neither *Mantra* nor *Tantra*.

Apart from the translated works in the Kanjur and Tanjur collection there are numerous original Tibetan Buddhist works on various subjects, such as medicine, history, philosophy, drama, dance, and even novels. Those original Tibetan works were compiled by well-known authors, such as Tsongkhapa, Milarepa Kunchen Jamyanshadpa, Gunthang Rinpoche, etc., just to mention a few. A list of all those authors would perhaps fill a book of the size of the '*Ramayana*'.

Today we can still find a vast amount of such original

Tibetan works that were written by both, Mongolian and Tibetan scholars, in spite of the socio-religious rules that governed Tibet for centuries. Those rules did not allow a secular book to be written. All compositions had to be confirm with the Buddhist *Dharma*. Even for writing Buddhist books three prerequisites were to be fulfilled: (1) Having the full ability of writing, (2) having obtained permission through a prophecy of one's tutelary deity that this work should be of benefit for all living beings, and (3) having obtained permission from the supreme head of one's school of thought whose office had the power of editing and checking the contents and their confirmity with the Buddhist law, prior to any publication. These rules are the reasons why there is almost no secular writing to be found in classical Tibetan literature.

Opposing those rules led to certain sanctions, and in those days society would have ignored such writings anyhow. Such incident happened to the famous contemporary Tibetan scholar from Amdo, Gedun Choephel, who entered India along with Rahul Sankrityayana on one of his Tibet journeys in the 1930s, and later worked with Dr. George Roerich at Urusvati in Kullu.

Gedun Choephel published one of his works, "The flower of Nagarjuna's Philosophy" , in India, outside the traditional rules for Tibetan compositions. In his work we find a critical account on Nagarjuna and Tsongkhapa, the founder of the Gelukpa School, to which Choephel belonged. For apparently no other obvious reasons, Gedun Choephel was taken into custody and suffered severe difficulties which finally led to his death. This happened in the 1950s.

Since then, things have changed, also for the Tibetan community, and new publications of Tibetan literature, also on modern subjects, are available in India and abroad.

Lepcha Studies and Some Social Values Evaluated

5

Arpita Chatterjee

The Lepchas are a race of Mongoloid stock who inhabit the southern and eastern slopes of Mount Kanchend-zonga in Sikkim, Darjeeling and Kalimpong. They are considered to be the earliest inhabitants of Sikkim. There is no fixed or accepted theory as to the origin of the Lepchas, but they themselves are generally of the opinion that the home of their ancestors—the people of Mayel—is one of the inaccessible valleys of Kanchendzonga. The language in its turn belongs to the Sino-Tibetan family of languages, and thus has an important link with the Tibetan stock.

In Sikkim, the Lepcha language is next to Nepalese and Sikkimese in order of popularity. Nepalese is understood by almost all except those in the far north; Sikkimese is spoken by the Bhotias and Lepcha is spoken only in the interior of Jongu where Lepcha villages are situated. However, the Lepcha language is the one that is indigenous to the state of Sikkim as it is the language of the earliest inhabitants.

The Lepcha people are highly distinct and different from their neighbours; they speak a different language and have a written corpus of hundreds of old manuscripts. Yet these have never been seriously investigated, regrets P. Klafkowski in his article "A Few Words on the Rong (Lepcha) Heritage".

This creates a major difficulty in studying much about the Lepchas.

However, we find Christian Missionaries have indirectly contributed to Lepcha studies, within a span of twenty seven years, from 1845 to 1872 W. Start, C. G. Niebel and others translated the Gospel of St. John, the Gospel of St. Mathew, Book of Genesis and Exodus and others into the Lepcha language. These missionaries of the past knew the language they were translating into. As a result, we get a first hand insight into the language of the Lepchas.

G. B. Mainwaring authored "A Grammar of the Rong (Lepcha) Language. As it exists in the Darjeeling and Sikkim Hills" , 1876 (reprinted in 1971), and a "Dictionary of the Lepcha Language". These are perhaps the earliest of scientific explorations into the language of the Lepchas as also their culture in general.

H. Siiger has listed the available western publications on Rong studies. It contains the basic bibliography. "The Lepchas, Culture and Religion of a Himalayan people" (Copenhagen, 1967) is a 3 Volume book by H. Siiger, J. Rischel and others. These volumes deal with social and cultural anthropology (V I), a selection of annotated and translated Rong religious texts (V II) and an analysis of Rong religion (V III).

Klafkowski has a number of writings of considerable value, such as "But They Don't Have Any Literature or A Few Words On The Rong (Lepcha) Heritage" ; "Towards A Rong-Tibetan Comparative Project" ; "Rong, The Vanishing Language and Culture of Eastern Himalayas" and others. In his last work we find a complete chronology of the Rong language text books printed in Darjeeling and Kalimpong.

R. K. Sprigg has a few important as well as interesting papers on some minor aspects of the language. We have some anthropological papers by Nebesky-Wojkowitz ; "Living with The Lepchas" , by John Morris ; "A Grammar of the Lepcha Language" , by B. N. Shah and of course G. Gorer's "Himalayan Village".

We also find some later writings like K. P. Tamang's "Lepcha Grammar" (in Rong only), Kalimpong, 1977, and A. Chakrabarty's "Read Lepcha" , 1977.

Gorer's Himalayan Village is specially worth mentioning again due to its exhaustiveness of information on the domestic and social life of the Lepchas. In fact, it deals with almost every possible aspect of the Lepcha people. This is not the case with many other ethnic group of the Himalayas where our knowledge is still lacking and wanting.

Gorer first published the book under the title *Himalayan Village ; An Account of the Lepchas of Sikkim,* 1938, which was later reprinted in 1984. This book has seventeen chapters which deals with a host of social and cultural facets of the Lepchas ; their home, their food, economy and trade, law and order kinship and marriage, religion (viz. Bon and Buddhism), birth, childhood, adulthood and death as well as other aspects of their life.

The different works and studies on the Lepchas have revealed them to be mainly Buddhists by religion, but they practise simultaneously other contradictory religions too. This in spite of the fact that the Buddhists and the Bons are agreeable on many points and are disagreeable on others. Their level of religious tolerance is obviously very high as the peaceful co-existence of the different religions seems to suggest and indicate.

Even though the Tibetans from the plateau largely succeeded in converting the Lepchas into Buddhists, the latter kept their separate identity. Their hold on the old faith remained strong and they often went to the local priest (Mun) for religious solace.

For a remote tribe in the confines of the Himalayas, the Lepchas have developed a surprising sense of cohesion and healthy social outlook. Villages are mostly self sufficient and to a large extent self governed even though the kazis do have their hold. Subtle recognition to the equality of the individual is given and there is no evidence of male domination. There is a healthy awareness of the needs of the individual, family and society. The Lepcha community of today is still fraught with supernatural beliefs of the pre-Buddhist days. In fact, certain peculiarities of their earlier faith are prevalent even while practising a more rational faith.

Perusing the different studies on the Lepcha people, we find them to be amiable and cheerful in dispositions. They are intelligent with an enquiring bent of mind but are generally timid and initially shy of strangers. They are spoken of as "the free, happy, laughing, and playful, no caste, Lepchas, the children of the mountains, modest, social and joyous in disposition".

Though simple and easy going by nature, the Lepchas are hardy people. Life, while making them strong, has also given them a wonderful understanding and appreciation of the different strains of the flora and fauna that nature has so abundantly surrounded their dwellings with.

They mix with equal ease both amongst themselves and with other people. There is a proverb which says that the Lepchas are like brass-pots, which are used equally in every household of all castes and classes. Like these brass-pots the Lepchas too mix easily with the low and high castes. The result is that the Lepchas of ethnic purity are rapidly decreasing and they are getting absorbed amongst the people with whom they live.

Expectantly, till very recently, the Lepcha language fell in disuse, and the culture shrouded in obscurity. The language did not find a place even in basic academic curricula. Things have, however, started looking up. After the merger of the State of Sikkim with the Union of India, the language is receiving its due attention and importance. It is being taught in schools. The Directorate of Education has taken the initiative of publishing books in Lepcha language. More and more such exposure to the language will undoubtedly open up the scope for better and more systematic studies on the Lepcha people in general and their culture in particular. Present day Tibetan studies will, thus, enable itself in expanding its wings to the people and culture of stocks not necessarily confined to the Tibetan plateau only.

References

1. G. A. Grierson, *Linguistic Survey of India*, Delhi, 1927, VIII, part I.
2. G. Gorer, *Himalayan Village: An Account of the Lepchas of Sikkim*, Delhi, 1984.
3. J. Morris, *Living with the Lepchas*.
4. P. Klafkowski, *On the Rong (Lepcha) Heritage*. (Contributions on Tibetan Language, History and Culture. Proceedings of the Csoma De Koros Symposium, Vienna, 1981).
5. N. Naresh, The Lepchas of Sikkim. (*Bulletin of Tibetology*, Sikkim Research Institute of Tibetology and other Buddhist Studies, Gangtok, 1982, No. 2).

A Glimpse of the Tibetan Lexicography

6

Kalpika Mukherjee

The idea that the Tibetan studies are essentially concerned with the Buddhist literature and that which does not have a Buddhist flavour remains outside pale is prevalent amongst people. May be due to the inaccessibility of this 'Forbidden Land'surrounded by the snowy mountain peaks of the Himalayas, people did not have much idea about this Highland.

As per record it is during the reign of one of the most illustrious and enlightened kings of Tibet—Srong btsan sgam po that Tibet had an opportunity of being acquainted with its neighbouring countries ; such as, rgya nag (China), rgya gar (India), bal yul (Nepal), li yul (Khalan) Khotan etc. He was not only credited with introducing Buddhism in Tibet but Tibet became culturally enriched under his patronship. Minister Thon mi sambhoṭa was sent to India to devise Tibetan scripts which replaced the primitive way of representing Tibetan language. Then Thon mi sambhoṭa also composed two grammars of Tibetan. Since then the world became curiously conscious about this land of Snow, a new era began in the cultural history of Tibet by the exchange of scholars with the neighbouring countries especially with India. India's cultural background, its literature and religion especially Buddhism had a great bearing on the Tibetan mind.

The Tibetans tough by nature, due to the topography and climate were essentially traders by profession and as such they had a wide range of access to the Asian Countries. Once the lower silk route was under the stronghold of the war-like Tibetans. The Tibetans had an opportunity to be acquainted with the culture and civilisation of its neighbouring countries since old days. The seventh century onwards Tibet became attracted with the different branches of Indian studies. In the monasteries the learned lamas proficient in Sanskrit language engaged themselves in translating the various Sanskrit texts on diverse subjects, besides the texts on Buddhism. Often this task was done in collaboration with the Indian Paṇdits. Also many indigenous commentaries were composed by the Tibetan scholars on many valuable texts. Only a few out of the non-Buddhist texts translated into Tibetan and preserved in the Tibetan btsan gyur collection is mentioned below:

1. *Subhāsita-ratna-karaṇḍaka-kathā*—legs par bshod pa rin po che za ma tog lta bu'i gtam
2. *Meghadūtam*—sprin gyi pho ña
3. *Nāgananda-nāṭakam*—klu kun du dgaṭ ba shes bya ba'i zios gar
4. *Cāndra vyākaraṇa* of Candragomin—lung ston pa tsandra pa'i mdo
5. *Amarakosa*—chi ba me pa'i mdzod with its commentary Kāmadhenu—dod 'jo'i ba mo

Also treatises on *chandas, nītishastra*, even music and various other books in different subjects were translated.

The greatest contribution of the Tibetans lies in the fact that they have preserved in translations many valuable Sanskrit texts originals of which in India were lost due to several reasons. Thousands of Tibetan Lo tsa bas in collaboration with the Indian Pandits worked on this mission. It was an extremely difficult task and for this the Lo tsa bas were required to possess a thorough knowledge of the Sanskrit grammar and lexicons. For the sake of uniformity bi-lingual lexicons were prepared at an early date. The learned Lamas met in conferences (chos'dus) to ensure that the translators attempted the exact rendering of the Sanskrit texts. The terminologies established by the learned Lo sta bas were approved by the Tibetan government and severe structures were awarded to those who transgressed the approved meanings. Especially the technical terms of the Buddhist literature were to be rendered with great caution. Let us take for example the word *dharma* derived from the root *dhṛ*-to hold, and each and everything that helps an individual to his constant becoming is *dharma. Dharma* denotes multiple meanings in different contexts; for example, *dharmāraṇya, dharmāsana, dharmādhikaraṇa, svadharma* and the like. Tibetan word for *dharma* is 'chos'—derived from 'bco ba' the future form of the root 'chos ba' to make, make ready, to build, to construct. 'Chos' means religious doctrine or religion, especially the religion of the Buddha. Generally speaking, 'chos' consists of all phenomena, all matter and all knowledge of things, worldly as well as spiritual. It includes 'shes bya'—all that can be known, 'shes bya'—all that is cognisable by the senses; all that exists and 'ghi grub' the basis and the material (1) 'chos' refers to 'chos lugs', *dharmaniyama* and chos lugs ston pa'i bslab ca'is the way of instruction of the shastra the regulator of *dharma.* Here 'chos' means *dharmavinaya* 'chos' lugs ston pa'i dpe cha'i ming. Another meaning of *dharma* is 'phyi rol yul nas thams cad kyi spyi min la chos zer'. This point refers to the Sarvāstivādī conception of *dharma* which is the general name for all that exists. (2) *Dharmatā* is the relation between the functionality of a phenomenon and its characteristics. The relationship between these two is in a constant flux. For example, the intrinsic nature of water is coolness, *swaitya, pica* its *kriyākāritva* or functionality is to flow down—*plavatā.* The correlation between these two is the *dharmatā* of water. This has been explained as—'chos ñid ni phyi yul na rang zhin gis gnas pa zhig yin stabs'. With reference to the different aspects of this functionality it has the capability of becoming and also all the functionalities of a phenomenon expands in all quarters and thereby *dharmatā* means the natural disposition or the very temperament of a phenomenon. Thus in a general way it may be said that because it adheres to the very nature of a phenomenon, it can hardly be worked out by understanding or intellect, 'mi blo bzo byed du med pa zhig yin'.

Then *dharma* means, in the ordinary sense of the term any practice or custom that is peculiar to a particular place. This is known as the *deshadharma*—'gtan tshig rig pa'i nag du rtcod pa'i gshi de la'ng chos zer te'. It has three parts viz (a) *sādhya dharma*—bsgrub bya'i chos', (b) *dharmi*—chos 'idan'and (c) *dharmalakṣaṇa*—'rtags chos'.

Dharma may also mean the ten religious practices. These are:

1) *Lekhana*—yi ge 'bri ba—writing
2) *Pūjana*—mchod pa—worshipping
3) *Dāna*—sbying pa—almsgiving
4) *Shravaṇa*—ṇyan pa—hearing
5) *Vacana*—klog pa—reading
6) *Udgrahaṇa*—'dzin pa—perceiving
7) *Prakasāna*—rab tu ston pa—instructing others
8) *Svādhyāya*—kha do 'don byed pa—repeating in loud voice.
9) *Cintana*—sems pa—meditation
10) *Bhāvanā*—sgom pa—recollection

To come back to the point, it is for this reason that of all the branches of the Tibetan studies lexicography demands utmost importance, since on this depends the correct interpretation of the original Sanskrit texts. Amongst all the bilingual lexicons the *Mahāvyutpati* (bye brag tu rtogs par byed pa) deserves first mention. It is known to all with what infinite pains Csoma de Körös prepared the first manuscripts of this vocabulary. In one of his reports to Capt. Kennedy, the then Assistant Political Agent, he writes—'This vocabulary arranged after certain matters or subjects under general heads, contains many thousand words of every description: several distinctions and divisions highly interesting in order to understand better the whole system and the principles of Buddhist doctrine'. This encyclopaedic work was originally composed with a view to standardizing the translational Tibetan. King Srong btsan sgam po (expired in 615 A.D.) is said to have encouraged the translations of the indigenous Indian texts. But this work could not have been effectively done until the Bsam yas monastery was established in the 8th century A. D. For about one hundred years the translations were not satisfactorily done. King Khri srong sde btsan felt the necessity of inviting a council of scholars from India to promulgate the translational work. In this context the 'Sgra 'byor' into two parts may be referred to.

However, the *Mahāvyutpatti* is the only bilingual dictionary in a joint venture. It started under the patronship of king Khri srong sde btsan and was completed under the supervision of his successor king Gtsug lde btsan (Ral pa can 815 A.D.) On the Indian side there were Acārya Jinamitra, Shilendrabodhi, Surendrabodhi and Bodhimitra; on the Tibetan side there were Ācārya Ratnarakṣita, Dharmashila and Lo tsa ba Mañjushrīvarman, Ratnendrashīla, Jñyānarakṣita and Jñanasena (ye shes sde).

Then there is the Tibetan rendering of the *Amarakosa* and its commentary *Kāmadhenu* by Subhuticandra. Pandita Shrīdharasena's *Abhidhānavacanakosa* of the Sa skya scholar

Mañjughoṣha ('jam dbyangs) and the encyclopaedic work *Shatasāhasra-sasana* (bk''bum), compiled by two well-known Sa skya scholars one of whom was Manjughosa may be mentioned. The *Dharmasamgraha* (Chos yang dag par bsdus pa)—a collection of Buddhist technical terms is attributed to Ācārya Nāgārjuna ('phags pa klu sgrub) regarding whose identity opinion differs. The *Prajna* or 'Shehrab' was compiled at a later date (1771 A.D.) by Btsan 'dzinr gyal mtshan. The work in the xylograph is divided into 14 parts of which I, III and V have been published by the Sikkim Research Institute of Tibetology, Gangtok in 1992. The dictionary compiled by Ray Bahadur Sarat Candra Das is indispensable to any learner of the Tibetan language. We know of the voluminous *Tibetan Sanskrit Dictionary* of Lokesh Candra and also of Jäscke. Sarat Candra Das mentions some Tibetan lexicons such as 'Theg chog mdzod', Mngon brjod mkhas pa'i rna rgyan' etc. Recently a Tibetan lexicon compiled by L. S. Dagya at Dharamsala. The unilingual dictionary *Dag yig gsar bsrgrigs* has been compiled by Mi nyung ba and has been published from Peking in 1973.

It is evident from this paper that the most essential branch of the Tibetan study which had started during the seventh century out of bare necessity continues even today with an uninerrupted way.

References

1. Preface to the *Tibetan-Sanskrit Dictionary* by Lokesh Candra.
2. *Tibetan-English Dictionary with Sanskrit Synonyms* by Ray Bahadur Sarat Candra Das, Published by Motilal Banarsidas, 1983.
3. *Sasrava-anasrava dharmah*; Vijnaptimatratasiddhi of Vasubandhu.
4. *Collected Works of Alexander Csoma de Koros-Sanskrit-Tibetan-English Vocabulary*, Gaurav Publishing House, New Delhi.

Bibliography

1. *Prajna*-Pub. by Sikkim Research Institue of Tibetology, 1992.
2. *Dharmasamgraha* of Acarya Nagarjuna, Kendriya Uccha Tibbati Siksa Samsthana, Sarnath, Vąranasi.
3. The *Dharmasamgraha*-Kenjiu Kasàwara Edt. by F. Max Muller, Cosmo Publications, New Delhi 1981.

Tibetan Language in Three Decades (1960-1990)

7

Anandamayee Ghosh

The study of the Tibetan Language with its Linguistic purview was innovated by the western scholars like Desgodine (1989), Laufer (1987), Forrest (1965) in the context of Sino-Tibetan Speech in Asia.

According to the Chinese tradition a group of people had resided in the Loess in between the Yangtze and the Huang Ho rivers. They migrated downwards and subsequently entered in North China.

The early inhabitants of the Huang Ho river valley towards the lower course of Huang Ho river and subsequently a group among them are said to have moved towards Yar lungs Gtsang po valley in Tibet.

The speeches of the Dogmi (nomads) and Gurpa (tent livers) of stod bod and those of sog po (the Mongols) of Coconor have contributed a lot in the growth of the Tibetan Language as spoken and written today.

The present study is limited within the periodical periphery of the last three decades (1960-1990) when the language geography of Tibet has extended in two opposite directions.

1. Towards north direction of Tibet in people's Republic of China (PRC).

2. To southern direction and India.

Furthermore a section of Tibetan speakers spread all over the world after being thrown away from their native land.

The identification of Tibetan language is late though Bon Po Priests claim the Zhang Zhung had been in vogue in west of Tibet when the Bon Po settlement spread in Guge, Brudza, Purang. Bod Skad, present name Tibetan (Poka) is said to have been systematized by Thonmi Sambhota in seventh century A. D. Some glimpses have been focussed since Zhang Zhung language texts have come down to us with its vocabulary list and its corresponding Tibetan rendering. Despite that the Tibetan could spread in East Asia, Central Asia since seventh Century A. D.

The spread of the Tibetan language in different parts of Asia has different dimensions. Tibetan had been strong in their material merchandise in Central Asia since seventh century A. D. The small estate or garrisons of Central Asia were captured by the Tibetans. Such military movement opened a new vista of the spread of Tibetan upto 9th Century A.D.

The classical Tibetan based on the Buddhist scriptures entered late there and that continued till the acceptance of Islam in central Asia through Semitic people of Arab. Obviously the language had been the primary means of communication in those areas and that extended upto Dung Huang. From seventh century downwards the extension of the language has been variegated as well as wider.

After the downfall of Btsan kingship (10th Century A.D.) the warring expansion of the Tibetans was checked, but the extension of the language had a continuous growth through several changes.

Again the close relationship between the Yuan rulers in China with the Sakya hierarch opened a new vista of language mobility in two fold directions: (i) Tibetan entered into Peking court and (ii) Mongolia with the garb of spiritual resources in understanding Buddhism. Several Tibetan monks went to Mongolia and translated the Kanjur (the sayings of Buddha) and Tanjur (the teachings of the eminent disciples of Buddha).

In addition to that several didactic lessons of the eminent Buddhist teachers of Tibet entered in Mongolia and those exhibit the wide spread of Tibetan in Mongolia. As a result of that a large number of Mongolian scholars (Mon. Hutugutu) endeavoured to compose in Tibetan.

On the other hand the Bhotias who had migrated from trans Himalayan land of snow (gans yul i. e. Tibet) in several occasions have been Indianized and Indian constitution accepts them as by name of Bhutia or Bhotia. They had distinct culture traits and their speeches belong to Tibeto-Burman group as the census report records.

In Sikkim an endeavour is observed to develop the Bhotia language though it is off-shooted from Tibetan. In the wide range of the Himalayas the speeches of the Bhotias have been accepted as the state language by the name of Bhotia in Sikkim and Ladakh in Jammu and Kashmir. As a result of that the latest trend of literature in Sikkim and Ladakh may go at par with the other literatures in India.

Among the Pemako, a section of Bhotia of Arunachal Pradesh hold that they crossed the Himalayas after being led by Guru Padmasambhava (8th century A. D.). However the Bhotias in general reside in the altitude of 6000 ft. or above of the mid Himalayas. They are heterogeneous but they had the common speech genera belonging to Tibetan.

As regards the spoken language of Bhotias who had migrated from Tibet and settled in India variation in vocabularies and their pronunciation and intonation from Tibetan standard language (Utsang) are observed. Grierson has elaborately stamped the variations.

Bhutia being off-shoot from Tibeto-Burmese group of the Sino-Tibetan speech family among the Asian Languages, it has some commonness with bod skad or Tibetan.

Since 1960 a sizeable number of Tibetan speaking people led by H. H. the Dalai Lama XIVth, Tanzin gyatso had crossed the Himalayas in southward direction of Tibet. The Tibetan language has thereby extended southward as those Tibetan speaking people are in India for taking political asylum.

From the language point of view the immigrant Tibetans speak various dialects of Tibetan. Regarding the dialects spoken by the migrant Tibetans, some Tibetan Scholars made an exposer on the latest trend in Tibetan (stod-skad, Hor-skad, dbus skad, khams-skad, Amdo-skad).

Despite that the literary Tibetan (gzhung-skad) continues with its basic structure. Gzhung skad is not the chos skad, the spiritual language used by the Buddhists or Bon po teachers. Also Gzhung skad is not the same as phal skad, spoken language. Gzhung skad in Tibetan has been popularly written from its spiritual garb. It is to note that the Gzhung skad tends to integrate both the migrant Tibetans and the Bhotia speakers on the literary level.

Another scenario of the Tibetan language since 1960 requires a brief elaboration. Since the establishment of People's Republic of China (PRC) led by Communist Party of China (CPC) a new directive regarding the speeches spoken by the minorities in Tibet Autonomous Region (TAR) and the Inner Mongolian Region (IMR) and Hunang Autonomous Region (HAR) of China and other was accepted by the language reform policy of China. As a result of that a new trend in Tibetan is observed. The National Council of the CPC adopted the following measures.

i) Use of Chinese vocabularies either in Tibetan transcription or in Tibetan rendering of the modern ideological terms e. g. C. di Gou Zhu i. E. imperialism. C. guan lian Zhu i. E. bureaucracy. (C=Chinese, E=English)..

ii) Adoption of vocabularies of the modern science, technology, geography etc. by their translations in compounded agglutinative structure e. g. . C. tan Ke. E tank C. Chi Cheng Kung E. technician. As a result of that new phonemes have been added in Tibetan in the recent change.

iii) Moreover, the spoken language got a new exposer to communicate the ideas and to change the views with the innovation of new diction and style of presentation i. e. modern construction of Chinese Syntax as used by the Tibetan speakers.

Such admixture in the language traits have extended rapidly in the Eastern Tibet and spread towards North East upto Beijing.

Besides the uses of dictions in the literary language gzhung skad. C. Wenxue de yuyan as distinct from Chos skad C. Sheng dian de yuyan, the structural change in morphology and syntax has opened an approach in Tibetan spoken in PRC.

By the three decades a new generation of the Tibetan speakers have grown up who had very little base of the pre 1960 Tibetan an account of the modern educational exposer disseminated by the authorities of the TAR of China.

The specimen of the present day Tibetan literary language are observed in the journals, periodicals and the popular works published from PRC.

On the basis of the above analysis it is evident that the Tibetan language in the Trans-Himalayas have undergone a drastic change from their ancestral pattern. However, the modernization of culture as well as socio-political aspects leave a room to innovate a new language pattern in TAR of China which is distinct from that of spoken by the Tibetans residing outside.

The growth of a language may be compared with a course of a river that runs different bends, left and right. The Tibetan language therefore has a wide boundary and that speaks about the wonders which the Tibetans possess. Tibet is strategically important in mid-Asia and therefore the extension of the language among the multi-ethnic groups hold the importance in the Asian-culture.

A language can never be restricted by a barrier nor a barrage. It has a flow of its own. The time would be the best judge to appreciate the endeavours done by the scholars.

Bibliography

1. Bai Shoyi, *An Outline History of China,* Beijing, 1982.
2. Forrest, A. D., *The Chinese Language,* London, 1965.
3. Par Karvern, *The Bonpo and Zhang Zhung language,* OSLO, 1958.
4. Pathak, S. K, *Society and Culture of the Himalayas,* Himalayas Research and Cultural Foundation. India 1995.
5. *Zhang Zhung Dictionary,* Solan. Himachal Pradesh.

Contribution of Guru Padmasambhava on Spread of Buddhism in Sikkim

8

Dechen D. Dorjee

This is the true and accurate account of the creations and accomplishments of Guru Padmasambhava in the Bayuol Demozong, the Hidden Land of Sikkim.

I bow to the feet of the Buddhas three times and the ten directions who abide in the heavenly paradise that is as expansive as the sky and to the prince *bodhisattvas* and the six ornaments. I pay my homage to them with a thousand spoked wheel of *Brahmas*. I especially make this offering to the holder of all the Buddha activities of the three times, the unequated one who was born miraculously from the lotus in the lake radiating thousands of rays of light. The Indestructible Lotus Born One. Please bless us. This is my homage.

Our greatest teacher, the extraordinary Buddha, predicted the birth of future Buddhas. The Buddha said in the *Mahaparinirvana Sutra,* "Eight years after I pass away, in the Lake of Donakosa, one who is even more excellent than me will be born". This is according to the Sutra. From the Tantra of Lamed Dhonzog, "Eight years after the *Parinirvana* of the Buddha, one who is Supreme will come to the world of Urgyen and he will be called Padma Jung Nay. The tradition of Tantra will be taught". Thus the appearance of Guru

Padmasambhava has been predicted in many Sutras and Tantras.

During the eighth century, the incarnation of *Man-ju-sri,* Trisung Detsen, the king of Tibet invited Guru Padmasambhava and Maha Pandita Shantarakshita to Tibet. These two great saints built the monastery of *Samye Mingyur Lhundredrup* which was the first of its kind in Tibet. The king also invited one hundred and eight great pandits including Vimalamitra. The complete teachings of *Dharma* from India was translated into Tibetan. As is well documented in many texts and histories, he made Tibet famous for being the paradise of *Buddha Dharma.*

What was the condition of Bayuol Demozong before the visit of Guru Padmasambhava? The land of Demozong had never been visited and blessed by the Buddha Sakyamuni. It was a barren land, full of rocks and empty valleys, infested with thick forests and difficult to travel through. There were no human habitants. It was rather inhabitated by wild monkeys, leopards, tigers, gorillas, bears and other wild animals who roamed the land. Samsaric gods, evil spirits and untamed deities lived in the land. The spirits of the cliffs, rocks, water and the nagas made it a dangerous and frightening place. In the eighth century, the time to spread the light of *Dharma* to this land had come and also the one who is the subjugator of all the evils, the miraculous and supremely powerful one who subjugated all the evil doers, the antidote to all evils, Guru Padmasambhava came to Sikkim. He visited the whole land, blessed it and proclaimed this hidden land as the most exulted place similar to the Copper Coloured Paradise. He named this land as, "Heavenly Celestial-*Khey Chos Palkyi Demozong*". He made it widely known to the whole universe and opened the sacred doors to the hidden land.

How did the *Buddha Dharma* spread in such a Land? I will explain how the *Dharma* spread in the beginning, the middle and the later periods. In the beginning of the spread of the *Dharma* tradition, the King of Tibet, Trisung Deutsen, his ministers and the people in one voice asked Guru Padmasambhava, "Oh Great Teacher, *Pema Jungney*, at the end of five hundred years, when the good tradition declines and bad activities become wide spread, all the countries will fight amongst themselves and many bad omens will occur. Countries will be in turmoil with negative views. China, Tibet, Mongolia and the strong armies will fight among themselves and the entire scene will become ravaged and poor. At that time what should we do?" Guru Padmasambhava said, "In the future when Tibet becomes ravaged and destroyed, I will point out the direction to which you can go to help the future generations have courage during that time of human sufferings".

The Guru gave the address and road-map of that sacred land. He taught the teachings to the people to practice when they go to the hidden land. "In future there will be the supreme place of Demozong for you all to run away to. Go there and perform the traditional ceremonies for the peace of Tibet and endeavour and persevere in your meditations. And thereafter Tibet will become peaceful".

How did the King, the Ministers and his people come to this hidden land ? "Oh great Teacher, please show us in reality the great exalted paradise that is like the Copper Coloured Mountain? "With miraculous power, Guru Padmasambhava took all the subjects and the king to the centre of the hidden land called "*Trakkar* (white rock) *Tashiding*. Included in the itinerary were *Khen-Lob-Choe-Sum,* Twenty five disciples, 108 Indian pandits including Vimilamitra and 108 translators including Vairochana. At Tashiding, Guru Padmasambhava gave the empowerment of Lama Gondue and other extensive teachings. The Guru gathered all the protecting spirits of

Demozong and through His spiritual power, He subjugated them and made them take vows to protect the *Dharma*. Some of the spirits were made the protectors of the land and some as protectors of "t e n m a".

Tashiding, the centre of the precious hidden land, still possesses the thrones of Guru Padmasambhava, the King and retinue. The rocky thrones are adorned with the symbols of eternity, continuity and happiness. You can still see the letters, "*Om Ah Hum*" that were carved in the rocks by the spiritual power of Vimilamitra. The Guru said, "All of you gathered here—listen 'This land is the palace of Lama, Yeidam, Khandro and Pawos. The rocks, the caves, and the lands, the mountains and the trees are all palaces of gods. Each one of these is the abode of a Buddha. This land is the real paradise of the Buddhas".

In the four directions around Tashiding are four miraculous and extraordinary caves. In the east there is a cave called *Shar-Chok-Bhey-Phuk.* In the south there is *Khandro-Sang-Phuk.* In the west there is *Dechen-Phuk,* the cave of Great Bliss. In the north there *Lha-Rhi-Gnying-Phuk.* There are many small caves around the four great caves. In all the four great caves one will find naturally arisen statues of Buddha, vowels and consonants imprinted on the rocks. There are nine caves where one can attain complete spiritual accomplishments. There are thirteen caves where one can develop common attainments as well as many other caves where one can achieve attainments.

"There are eight rare *Ka-Gye* lakes, 109 precious lakes of protecting deities and 1000 other small lakes. This land is also called the land of medicine as there are many herbs that can cure diseases and rejuvenate the body. This land is also called a gold though for all types of fruits and vegetables can grow there. It is also called the palace of *Pema-Chen* as all varieties of flowers blossom in this place. Since all evils can be subjugated there, it is equal in spiritual power of *Dorje-Den*. It is also like the palace of Re-Potala as compassion and loving kindness arises naturally there. It is like *Riwo-Tse-Gna* in China because one's intelligence naturally can be developed in this land. When one meditates there, one attains power like in the palace of *Changlo-Chen*. In this land, the *Khandromas* actually gather similar to that of western land of *Odiyana*. Thus He proclaimed the great qualities of this land.

Middle Period

During the middle era, *Rigzing Chenpo Gyukyi Dem-Thrul-Chen* came with eight precious and sacred disciples. *Katok Lama, Yeshe-Bumpa, Sonam Gyaltsen* and many other great teachers came to this sacred land and began to practice the teachings of Buddha and attained accomplishments at Tashiding. They offered numerous and great offerings (tsoks) at Tashiding and thus began the special and auspicious time for *Demozong*. *Rig-zing-Go-Dem* opened the door to the sacred land. He established the practice of meditation and accomplishment at *Pawo-Hung-Rei*. He also reminded the protecting deities of their vows and admonished them to renew with greater vigour.

Later Period

It has been said in the treasure text of *Ter-ton Raetnalingpa* that "This land is the most supreme of all hidden lands. It is the heaven of the extraordinary ones". Like this he often praised the land of Sikkim. Owing to the collective good *karma* of all the inhabitants of this land, Guru Padmasambhava emanated there in later years in the forms of *yogis*. According to the treasure text of *Raetnalingpa*, the incarnate of the great Pandita, Vimilamitra, Lha-Tsun-Namkhar Jigme, came from the northern gate. Gnada-Sempa Phuntsok-Rigzing came from the western gate. Katok Kun-Tu-Zangpo came from.the southern gate. The king's lineage originated from the radiant gods. The Chogyal Phun-Tsok Namgyal came fron the eastern gate. These four saints met in 1642 at a beautiful place surrounded by trees and flowers, a garden of fruits, the center of all prosperity, the land of Yuksam. They met on a hill-top which is like a jewel. In order to start an auspicious cycle, they gathered samples of earth and stone from all over Sikkim and built a *stupa* called *Chang-Chub-Choeten-Tashi odBar* at *Norbu-Gang Yuksam.* At the time of consecration of the *stupa*, the sky was filled with a tent of rainbows and the whole land shown with rainbow coloured lights. All this was seen and experienced in reality by all the people. This was the sign of the beginning of the great era—the spread and practice of *Dharma* tradition and a new social order in Sikkim.

The great *Lhad-Tsun Chenpo* constructed the monasteries of *Drub-Dei* in Yuksam, *Sagnak Choeling, Pema-Yangtse* and many others. He established an order of monks and taught widely the Dzogpa Chenpo teachings in Sikkim. Gnadak Sempa Phuntsok Rigzing established monasteries called *Lha-Kang Marpo, Gsenun* and *Tashiding,* besides organising a community of practising monks in all these monasteries. He spread the *Dharma* far and wide. Through his spiritual power generated from reciting millions of times of *mantras* (manee), he was able to create vase (Bhumpa) of water. The water in that vase never decomposes or dries out. It rather remains fragrant and sweet. One can still see and feel the Vase. Thousands of devotees visit *Tashiding* to take blessings from the water contained in that miraculous and extraordinary vase every fifteenth day of the first month of Buddhist calendar. The nectar-like water from the vase is considered most auspicious.

Katok Rigzing Chenpo established *Dok-Gyun* monastery at Yuksam and Pakyong and organised an order of monks.

He disseminated the *Bhuddha Dharma* throughout the land. The Chogyal Phuntso Namgyal built a palace called *Tashi Tenkar* at Yuksam.

The great Lha-Tsun Chenpo exhibited his miraculous power by leaving a clear imprint of his foot on a rock at Yuksam. Katok Rigzing Chenpo also created a lake through his spiritual power. Both these places can still be seen today.

In summary, the precious *Dharma* tradition has spread and continues since the time of the great Yogis. We now have many monasteries where *Dharma* rituals and ceremonies are performed without interruption on the holy days. Once a year monastic dances and rituals are performed as part of the *Dharma* tradition and practice in almost all the traditional monasteries in Sikkim.

In 1964, the Chogyal of Sikkim, Tashi Namgyal, established an Institution called *Dre-Zong Gnagyur Sheydra Thubten Do-Gna Choeling* where one can study higher *Nyingma* philosophy. In this Institution, one can attain inner knowledge and get the degrees of Purba Madhyama to Acharya. This institute is affiliated with the S. Sanskrit University of Varanasi (U. P).

In conclusion, the great Teacher of Urgyen, Guru Padmasambhava actually visited the land of Sikkim in person. He walked throughout the land of Sikkim and blessed it. He opened the sacred sites and hid many *Dharma* treasures. The Guru entrusted the rare texts to the protecting deities and spirits and made them to take vows and oaths of protection. Several incarnates of Guru Padmasambhava visited the hidden land and extracted the hidden treasures in appropriate and auspicious days.

In order to practice, continue and disseminate *Buddha Dharma,* He established this hidden land as a place of forbearance and *Dharma* cultivation. He led countless sentient beings to the path of contentive liberation. His activities of enlightened kindness is beyond thoughts and description.

The Guru made Tibet, the land of snow mountains, famous for *Buddha Dharma*. The sentient beings of the present age are able to learn the Buddhist teachings as a result of His kindness. The rare and miraculous creations of the Guru are as deep as the ocean and as high as the entire sky.

In this instant presentation, I have been able to explain only a drop of what Guru Padmasambhava is all about.

Role of Padmasambhava in Tibet

9

Bela Bhattacharya

Buddhism entered Tibet during the reign of King Stron-btsan-Sgam-po (from 628-698 A.D). Under his royal patronage it flourished a little but under his immediate successors also Buddhism could not thrive greatly. But under the age of Khri-Sron-lde-btsan (755-797 A.D), Buddhism was firmly-established in Tibet and became in fact the state religion. This was principally due to the assistance the king received from the learned Indian teachers, like Padmasambhava, Santaraksita whom he invited to Tibet to spread the teaching of *Buddha* among his people.

Padmasambhava was a famous *Siddha* (perfect one) who is also regarded by some sects in Tibet as equal in status to the Lord Buddha. In the second half of the eighth century A.D., he was invited to go to Tibet from his homeland, which was probably is now the Swat area of Pakistan, to teach and advice on the foundation of the first Buddhist monastery in Tibet, (*Samye*). He created a great impression with his knowledge of Tantrism and tantric practices, then reaching their most developed form in India.

Amitabha emits a red ray of light that pierces the *Dhanakosa* Lake in *Oddiyana* and an immaculate lotus arises from the centre of the Lake. King Indrabhuti despatches his minister to find out miraculous emanation. The minister finds a child of eight, seated on the lotus, encircled by rainbow asuras and dakinis. When the child is brought to the court and the King asks him he replies: "My father is wisdom. My mother is voidness. Mine is the country of *Dharma*. I am sustained by clarity and perplexity". He is Padmasambhava. Like a second Buddha, Padmasambhava came into the world west of Bodhagaya in *Oddiyana* by apparitional birth. He is the *Dharmakaya* or absolute reality. He exhibits two kinds of supernatural forms: the pure, in which he appears in the divine and human realms, and the impure, in which he appears to the lower orders of beings. As the *HRIH* went out from the heart of Amitabha and settled on a lotus flower, an eight years old boy, endowed with all Knowledge, was born. After that he was seen by King Indrabhuti, who invited him to his palace adopted him as his son. Then he consecrated him as king. The people thereupon called him Padmavajra and Rajasekhara. When he was grown up, he realised that the world was devoid of reality and renounced his kingship. He then went to the cremation ground near Bodhgaya, which was a famous resort of Yogins, and gained emancipation of mind through the higher practices.

Padmasambhava sits with roses in *Vajrasana.* He holds a *Vajra* in the right hand and a skull in the left. The magic staff of *Khatvanga* rests in the crock of his left arm. The three are characteristics of great exorcist, of an eminent tantric master who vanquishes demons. By his magical power, which none could withstand, he subdued the demons or enemies of Buddhism in Tibet. He converted them and transformed them into protectors of the *Dharma*. Their new role as defensores fider made them ardent defenders of the faith, in their fear-inspiring character. The new world order was symbolised by the construction of the Samye monastery in 749, consecrated in the presence of Padmasambhava. Samye was to be the continuing symbol of Tibet as the *Buddha-ksetra.* He directed the translation of *Sutras* and *Mantras* brought from India. While Santaraksita represented argument and logic, Padmasambhava was the translogical thaumaturge. He was a powerful apostle of Tantricism. He visited mountains caves, snowpeaks, forests, lakes, and monasteries. He delivered teachings to many disciples, He also told the King that he would transform the land of Tibet into a rich land by his meditative power. He expounded to the Tibetans the fundamental teachings of Buddhism which received a good impetus there.

Padmasambhava abolished the practice of animal sacrifice used by the people in Tibet. He substituted instead the meal, rice and cake sacrifices known as Torma. Thus gradually arose the Buddhist worship with flour cakes common in Himalayan countries and Tibet. Padmasambhava married the sister of Santaraksita named Mandarava. According to Petech King *Kri-srong-lde-btsan* gave his daughter Khrom-la-rgyan in marriage to Padmasambhava. He was an eminent teacher in the University of Nalanda. He was deeply versed in the Tantricism of the Yogacara school of Buddhist thought. On the advice of Acharya Santaraksita, King Khri-srong-lde-btsan sent messengers to invite Padmasambhava to Tibet. He accepted the invitation. He was warmly welcomed by the King when he reached Tibet. Petech[1] thinks that the importance of the *bSam-yas* monastery is "undoubtedly exaggerated" by the Tibetans, his main arguments being that this importance is to be found specially in the *rGyal-rabs-ysat-ba'me-lon* written by *bsad-nam-rgyal-btsan* who was himself a monk of the *bSam-yas* and, therefore, was naturally inclined to exalt his own monastery.

Padmasambhava took initiative for building this monastery. According to the usual Tibetan accounts, after the local devils and demi-gods were subdued by Padmasambhava, he, along with Santarakshita, laid the foundation of the Sam-yas monastery, which, king Khri-Sron lde-btsan got, constructed. This means that Santaraksita was brought back to Tibet before the work on the bSam-yas monastery, started. From 'Gos Lo-tsa-ba's account, (in Roerich's translation), however, it is not clear whether Santaraksita returned to Tibet before the first initiative was taken towards the building of the monastery. According to Bu-ston[2] after Padmasambhava subdued the Tibetan demons, Santaraksita was invited to bSam-yas and established his residence there. "The acarya Bodhisattva in his turn, examined the ground, took the monastery of *Odantapuri* as a model and made a plan containing the forms of the mount Sumeru, the 12 continents, both the sun and the moon, all these surrounded by circumference of iron". bSam-yas was built according to this plan. From Bu-Ston's accounts, therefore, it appears that the first real initiative of the building of bSam-yas was taken by Santaraksita, though only after the great, exploits of Padmasambhava.

Waddell[3] asserts that the monastery was built in A. D. 749. This date is accepted by both P. N. Bose and B. Bhattacharya[4] though, curiously enough, on the authority of S. C. Das, [5] who actually says that the monastery was completed in the year called she-fire-hare. The two Fire-Hare years proximate to Khri Sron-Lde-btsan's reign were A. D. 787. The bSam-yas was the first Buddhist monastery. Many Buddhist temples built in Tibet from the time of Sron-btsan-sgam-po. He created a great impression with his knowledge of Tantrism and tantric practices, then reaching their most developed form in India. After his death he was deified and became the patron deity of the *Nyingmapa* (Red Hat) Sect. The *Nyingmapa* celebrate festivals of important events in the life of Guru rinpoche (Padmasambhava). Guru rinpoche as the Second Buddha of the *Nyingmapas*, must be distinguished from his aspect as the historical personage, the *siddha* Padmasambhava. he was a contemporary of Hayalila of

Oddiyana. He studied the *tantras* of all classes at Santirupa's school.

Padmasambhava set out for Tibet on the 15th day of the eleventh month of the Tibetan calendar. First he went to Nepal and remained there for three months as a guest of the King. When he came back from Nepal, *dakinis* and other spiritual beings begged him not to go to Tibet, but the Guru said that he must go as the time had come to subdue the evil spirits. He arrived in Tibet about three and a half months later, in A. D. 747, at the beginning of spring. He went to Tibet twice and stayed there for some years. His principal task was to demonstrate the superiority of the miracle-working power of Buddhism to that of Bon.

Padmasambhava advised to send a team of monks from Tibet to India to study the Buddhist works in the original Sanskrit. At the request of the King he selected a site for the monastery and Acharya Santaraksita consecrated it. With the construction of this monastery Buddhism made steady progress in Tibet. Gradually it became a great centre of Buddhist learning in Tibet. Some say that Guru Padmasambhava stayed in Tibet for six months or eighteen months while others say six years or twelve years. But many *NYing-ma-pa* and some non-*NYing-ma-pa* maintain that Padmasambhava was in Tibet for fiftyfive years and six months.

Pad-ma-bkah-than, the famous biography of Guru Padmasambhava, was discovered in 1326 by Urgyanlingpa from the Crystal Rock cave of Yarlung. It is the longest and the most comprehensive life of him.

The eight manifestations of Padmasambhava are as follows:

1. Urgyan Rdo rjc hchan, the *vajra dhara* of Urgyan
2. *Guru Sakya singe*, Guru Sakyasimha

3. *Padma-rgyal-po,* Lotus king
4. Padmasambhava.
5. *Blo-ldan-mchag-Sred,* The One Having Supreme Understanding of the World.
6. *Ni-ma-had-zer,* Rays of the Sun
7. *Rdo-rje-gro-lod,* Vajra Comforter of Beings.
8. *Sin-ge-sgra-sgrogs,* who Teaches with a Lions Voice.

Eight scrolls depict the eight manifestations. At the back of *Ni-ma-had-Zer* is the Mount Potala *Stupa* made of precious crystal.

At 8th century A. D., Padmasambhava procured a number of Buddhist texts from Kashmir, many learned monks were employed to render them into Tibetan. Vairocana was the best monk. Many Buddhist monks came to Tibet from Magadha to translate Buddhist texts into Tibetan.

Padmasambhava is known even to-day in Tibet as Guru or Mahacarya Padmasambhava. He is also called Guru Rinpoche and he is known as the first propagator of Buddhism in Tibet. He "was the greatest teacher and other teachers were the pupils and followers". He is highly respected in the religious history of Tibet. "As Guru Padmasambhava was the founder of Lamaism, and is now deified and as celebrated in Lamaism as Buddha himself than whom, indeed, he receives among several sects more worship, he demands detailed notice".[6]

Bibliography

1. *Aspects of Buddhist Culture from Tibetan Sources;* A. C. Banerjee, Firma KLM Private Limited, Calcutta, 1984.
2. *Buddhism & Lamaism of Tibet;* L. Austine Waddell, Heritage Publishers, New Delhi, 1974.

3. *The History of Buddhism in India and Tibet;* Bu-ston, Heidelberg, Leipzig, 1932.
4. *The Blue Annals;* George N. Roerich, Motilal Banarsidass, Delhi, Second Edition, 1976.
5. *2500 Years of Buddhism;* ed. by Prof. P. V. Bapat, Publications Division, Ministry of Information and Broadcasting, Government of India, 1971.
6. *Buddhism in India and Abroad;* A. C. Banerjee, The World Press Private Ltd., 1973.
7. *Tibetan Art;* John Lowry, London Her Majesty's Stationery Office, Victoria and Albert Museum, 1973.
8. *A Cultural History of Tibet;* Weidenfeld and Nicolson, 5 Winsley Street, London, 1968.
9. *Atisa and Tibet;* Alaka Chattopadhyaya, Calcutta, 1967.
10. *Tibet: Land of Snows;* Giuseppe Tucci, Oxford & IBH Publishing Co, Calcutta; Bombay, New Delhi, 1967.
11. *Transcendental Art of Tibet;* Lokesh Chandra, International Academy of Indian Culture and Aditya Prakashan, New Delhi, 1996.

References

1. Petech-70
2. Bu-ston II, 189.
3. Waddell, L 28.
4. Sec. H. B. I, 333n
5. S. C Das in *JBTS* I. I. 4.
6. L.A. Waddell, *Buddhism and Lamaism of Tibet*, p. 24.

Mask: A Significant Trait of the Tibetan Culture

10

Chittaranjan Patra

Masks or false faces have been used in religious and profane purposes since prehistoric times. The distribution of masks ranges widely over time and space. In some society masks play an important role in ritual activities. The pictorial representations of wearing of masks by the human beings occur in the cave paintings and rock engravings where dancers wearing animal masks.

The material shape of masks are of infinite variety. The masks were usually made of wood, metal, cloth, leather etc. The moulded or carved surface representing the interior half of the head and usually worn over the face of a person. Masks may be divided into two categories, the religious and the profane. The religious type of masks comprising a large number of sub-types, predominates in pre-literate socities as well as in several historic civilizations. The wooden masks surmounted by upright carved animal ears, deer horn represents the main form and by its crude shape and the painting in white, black and red creates a dramatic effect, such masks are used in connection with initiation rites, burial and other ceremonies. The task of covering these masks, which attract great magical powers, was considered highly dangerous and needed strength of the performers.

In ancient Tibet mask was known as *bse 'beg'*or "leather mask". It was also known as the *Tsiu dmar Icog dbug khang.* They represented only the 'Protecters of religion (*Chos—Skyong*), not just any deities. This was not fortuitous; masks probably share with mediums; the peculiarity of making it easier for the deities to become manifest. The miraculous image of turquoise, a lion crystal, a wooden bird, a leather mask (bse'bag) were some of the objects kept at the residence of Pe har at Bhata Hor (Tucci, *Painted Scrolls,* II p. 643). The most important medium of *Tsi'u dmar po* resides at *Samye* in the so-called *Tsi'u dmar, Icog dbug khang* where the ancient masks known as the *Srid pa'i smug chung* is being preserved. The mask is also to be found on the lower floor of *Samye* monastery in the *mgon khang*—the chapel where the worship of the dharmapalas takes place. A huge number of old masks, representing the faces of various protective deities, is being preserved in this monastery. Most of the masks are fastened to the horizontal beams forming a part of the ceiling. The *Srid pa'i smug chung* is, however, kept apart, thoroughly wrapped in cloth, inside a small wooden chest. This oldest mask is strictly prohibited to see for the public, only a few high dignitaries of the Tibetan state and monastery have been allowed to examine closely this sacred mask. According to A. de Riencourt (*Lost world: Tibet, Key to Asia,* London, 1950) the chest is said to have been opened for the last time when Rva Sgreng rin po che, the former Regent of Tibet, paid visit to *Samye*. The mask has an old appearance. It shows the face of a ferocious demon, with three eyes and a highly opened mouth.

The performance of 'Devil dances' has been made familiar from its occurrence in the Far-East. There it extends from China, through Tibet to Ceylon. Tibetan mask dance enjoys international reputation. This dance is popularly known as devil dance. This dance is performed in the premises of the monastery (Gumpha) by the lamas in the specific period of time connected with religious festivals. The lamas in the robe of both Gods and devil participate in the dance. Masks are widely used and the Lamas are given to entertainments in which the performers wear hideous masks, representing the demons of the underworld. The masks are in the form of men, beasts and ogres of hideous monstrosity. These demons are the nature-spirits which Tibetans worshipped before the introduction of Buddhism. Typical Tibetan musical instruments are played upon and the Choreography of the dance syncronizes with the war dance. The masks are most colourful and stylistically quite distinct. Masks of the demons are most fierceful. The masks as the head is the focus of the dance expressing the people's faith in fertility. Its use is to conceal the identity of the dancer from the crowd and its decoration the representation of the spirit evoked by it. Spirits represented in masks were credited with rather less wit to see through the masks than the average human. So in Tibet the masks have been mainly used in dramatic performances, both ritual and theatrical. The most notable examples of striking and elaborate masks are those worn by Lama-dancers in Tibetan temple festivals. Masks representing supernatural beings half-human and half-animal occur in Tibet. Like many primitive peoples, the Tibetans believe that animals as well as humans are animated by souls and that the barrier between them is slight. Their sculptured masks depict strange creatures with human faces and animal horns or beings combining the elements of men and animals. The ritual masks are widely used and the masks are mainly associated with the cult of ancestors and in the ritual of death. The aims of these rituals are to expel the spirits from a certain place and to maintain peace of the family of the dead person.

The masks employed in the devil dances are made of papier-mache, cloth and occasionally gilt copper. These masks are mainly of superhuman size, having a vertical diameter of at least twice the length of an ordinary human face, and a breadth in proportion. Each has projecting tusks and of an anthropoid form have a chaplet of five skulls, with predant bead ornaments of human bones. The masks represent divinities, demons, spirits, historical personages and allegoric figures.

The oldest mask of *Samye* (8th Century A. D) monastery was probably made of strips of cloth, which had been covered with glue and then pressed together, a technique sometimes applied for manufacture of Tibetan masks. It is also said that coagulated blood was used to make this mask.

The occupation of mask carver in Tibet is often handed down from Lama to Lama on accounts for a lot of indifferent work.

The masks are prepared by the Lama craftsmen strictly according to their religious concept. They are usually carved of wood, mashed paper and cloth and painted in varied colours and usually provided with a Yak-tail wing. When the masks are completed they are stored within the monastery under the custody of the Lamas to perform the dances in various festivals surrounding the monastery. The mask dancers are accompanied by the recitation of prayers and sacred texts.

The dresses accompanying the masks are as ample robes of rich brocade and satin, with gilt embroidery. The weapons carried by the maskers are made of wood carved with dorje patterns. The staves of the skeletons are topped by the head of a dead person.

In Tibet there are itinerant devil dancers, who go from village to village and from rest-house to rest-house giving imitations of the devil dances performed in the monasteries. These wanderers wear wooden masks of a traditional design. The masks which are frequently heirlooms, bear a far more pleasing expression than do the majority of those used at the lamasery dances. Round their waists the dancers wear girdles of Yak tails, which add greatly to the effect of their peculiar evolutions.

The ritual and dance provide occasion for the general expression of the people, binding them together socially in the ceremony of the common belief.

The rhythm of the drums calling the people to the monastery. As the common folk and Lamas approach, their walking gait bends to the drums beats. Tiny tots tied to mother's back respond with rocking shoulders. The traveller is tempted to cast reverse aside and take part on the periphery of humans ceremonially engaged in ecstatic ceremonial rejuvenation.

The layman see in the masked figures not so much lamas enacting gods and demons, but rather the mystic presence of the divinities and demons represented by the masks. In Tibet it was usual for the spectators to prostrate themselves before the masked figure of Gods and to solicit their blessing. The mystery play here assumes the character of an immediate interaction between man and supernatural powers.

In Tibet, sacred dramas illustrating the former births of the *Buddha* and similar events are performed by masked lay actors. A mystery play with manifestations of gods and demons by awe-inspiring masks is performed exclusively by the Lamas at particular seasons of the year and is still called "Dance of the *Red Ziger Devil*". This play appears to have been organised by a devil-dancing cult and is performed for the exorcising of demons.

At the Lamaist monastery of Choni, in Tibet, a devil dance takes place every September. During the dance a very peculiar ceremony is performed. A little figure of human shape, made of flour and dyed red, having been placed on the ground, is dismembered by one of the Lama and the fragments thrown among the spectators. This figure is an effigy of a false emperor of Tibet. At certain stages of the dance copper trumpets, some nine or ten feet long, are sounded, which, together with the other strange instruments of the orchestra, combine to make a terrific din. The old women regard the dance with greatest awe; the younger generation treat it as an amusing performance.

Mask dances (*Cham*) have been invented and are publicly performed partly to comic relief and partly to educate the lay-folk about religious messages and a bit of Tibetan history as well. *Cham* dance was provided by two masked dancers who kept the audience amused in the intervals between the dances. These dancers perform caricature of original Indian Pandits who had brought Buddhism to Tibet. The *cham* dances were performed to the accompaniment of music played by monk musicians. The monk performers were dressed in rich costumes of embroidered and appliqued silk brocade. If a monk was playing the part of a god or some other unearthly creature, he wore a fantastic painted mask.

"*Cham* dances" are also held before the performance of the military pageant. This portion of the celebration was symbolically presided over by *Ho-Shah*, the Chinese god of wealth. The role of *Ho-Shah* was played by a monk in a bigger-than-life-size mask of the god's head. This *cham* dance was performed during the New Year Celebrations at the Potala in Lhasa. The mask of the *Grul bum* (god of wealth) is a lion's head with a green mane.

"*Yama* dance" was also performed by the Tibetans. The masks worn by the dancers were far from amusing. The dancers were masked and costumed to represent the lords of the cemetery. The dance represent fearsome-looking skeletons. The bones of the skull seemed to protrude from the mask and the mask had a crown of skulls too. Masks like these were meant to be frightening in order to help the Buddhist meditator focus on and deal with his fears.

The mask dancers also represent the *Buddha*'s first sermon in the Deer Park in India. Here the words of the Master were said to have the power of a lion roaring. This dance is called the snow-lion. The Tibetan snow-lion dancer carried a sword, and his papier-mache mask, painted with brilliant colours, had a marvellously ferocious expression.

The Tibetan Lamas also performed deer dance. The deer mask was a combination of the slightly fearsome and the very fanciful. The deer masks were both heavy and very hot to wear. So the dancers wore knitted or felt caps to protect their shaven heads from irritation.

From the above discussion we may conclude that the purpose behind the mask is to protect from supernatural dangers and masks are and always were primarily means of transformation and identification with the entities of a non-material sphere to which man has access only if he sheds own identity and centres that of being existing on a superior plane.

References

1. Bell, Charles, *The People of Tibet*, Oxford, Carendon Press, 1928.
2. *Tibet, Past and Present;* Oxford, Clarendon, 1924.
3. Dalai Lama XIV, *My Land and My People* (English translation only), New York, Mc Graw-Hill Book Company, 1962.

4. David-Neel, Alexandra; *Magic and Mystery in Tibet*, New York, Claude Kendall, 1932.

5. Nebesky-Wojkowitz, Rene de; *Oracles and Demons in Tibet*, Gravenhage Mouton, 1956.

6. Rockhill, William Woodville; *The Land of the Lamas*, New York, The Century Co., 1891.

Non-violence and Nature Awareness in the Chos kyi tshi gs su bcad pa (Dhammapada)[1]

11

Malavika Bandyopadhyaya

The earth is not lonely, but is full of lives, especially the plants, animals and human beings are inseparately dependent on each other as the parts of the nature. Somewhere the human life is invisible, like dense forest, but other two cannot be exempted from anywhere. Nature is surrounded by these three lives, and these three are also fully alive in nature. They are aware of their living. So an individual through a particular process becomes aware of his own nature *(svabhāva*) and the characteristics of the worldly phenomena.

Gautama after renunciating his royal palace of Shākyas, in course of his formative life towards the attainment of *nirvāṇa*, endeavoured to be unified with the nature (Sanskrit-*prakrti*, Pali *pakati* or *nisarga*, Pali *nisagga*).

He spent six years of his strenuous life lonely like rhinoceros, *khaḍgoviṣāṇa* (Pali-*khagga visāna)*.[2] He was then an individual like a *pratyekabuddha* (Pali-*paccekabuddha)*.[3] After his attainment of the *nirvāṇa* he did appreciate the self nature of the truth where no violence was visible to him:

gang du gnas na las kyi mi tsugs pa'i
sa phyogs de ni yod pa ma yin te /
bar snang la med rgya mcho'i nang na med
ri bo rnams kyi gseb tu zhugs kyang min//[4]

On this earth therefore, every living being is born in the same home (eco) and is therefore to be looked upon with equity. Every being should be non-malignant. If any being becomes malicious for self-interest, there will be then no equality. Hence any harm done to others in self interest amounts to violence or *himsā.*

sdig pa byed pa rang nyid de
rang nyid kho nas nyon mongs byas /
sdig las ldog pa rang nyid de
rang nyid kho nas rnam par dag /
dag dang ma dag rang nyid de
gszhan gyis gszhan ni dag mi byed. //[5]

By oneself alone is evil done, by oneself is one defiled. By oneself is evil avoided, by oneself alone is one purified, purity and impurity depend on oneself. No one can purify another.

Indian traditions lay emphasis on nonviolence in respect of living beings which is regarded as the supreme virtue of the human beings (*ahimsā paramo dharmah, Mahābhārata, Vanaparva* 206/74), that means one should not be violent to others. This attitude is traced back to the Vedas which emphasises non-violence, for example "*ma himsyet sarvabhūtāni*". Here *sarvabhūtāni* means all existent beings whether animate or in-animate. All the *shrutis* (Vedic lore) and the *smṛtis* (subsequent social codes) are vocal in the same point.

Both Gautama the Buddha and Mahāvira the Jina followed the said legacy of no-nviolence, *ahiṃsā* or non-violence is the very basic concept in Buddhism as well as in Jainism. The seed of non-violence stands only on indignation and inadvertence in Jainism, Acarya Umasvami's indication of violence is, *"pramattayo gat pranavya pa ropanani himsa" (Tattvartha-sutra* 7/9). The same definition is accepted in the *Acaranga, Sutrakrtanga, Pravacanasāra* texts. Why non-violence is intently accepted, the Mahavira gave the answer.[6.]

Similarly the Buddha insisted on "*pānāti pāta veramaṇī*" some difference in approach regarding *ahimsa* may be noted in respect of a Buddhist and a Ja:na person. A Buddhist prescribes restriction from violence according to one's mental inclination while as the Jaina perspective tends to observe non-violence rigorously. That makes the Buddha's path, The Middle path *(madhyamā patipat).*

The seed of non-violence was in the self nature of the Buddha. The vibration of life is based upon non-violence. The dictum of the Buddha's welfare of beings is "*bhuta va sambhavesi va sabbe satta bhavantisukhitatta" (Suttanipata, Mettasutta 5).* According to *Samyuktanikaya* the definition of *himsa* is: *"yo kayena vacaya manasa ca na himsati sabbam ahimsako honti yo param na uihimsatiti".* (Brāhmaṇasutta, *Ahimsakasutta*).

Gaṇutama the Buddha prescribed that every person should look upon the other beings with compassion as a mother takes care of his only child (Samyukta Nikaya *Padasutta*). Gautama the Buddha endeavoured to win over violence by compassion.

In this connection a narrative regarding the life of the Buddha may be referred. Once a flock of sacred ducks was passing with unadulterated joy over the sky. Gautama the Buddha noticed their cheerfulness. Suddenly one of them had been stuck with an arrow and fell down on the ground. Shakyaputra picked up that very injured duck with compassion and gave back its life by throwing away the arrow.

In this way when he rescued the duck from its death, Devadatta, who had shot the arrow, came there with full demand of the 'duck for his arrow rightly aimed at'. To Devadatta such killing was a game when thousands of ducks were floating in the sky.

Shakyaputra became very sad and said that the life which was inside the duck, also was as same as that of a human being. Gautama's compassion aroused out of nonviolence as he was aware of the ecological self nature (*svabhava*), that is the nature awareness (*prakṛāti pratijāgaratā*). Non-violence and nature awareness are interrelated to preserve the equity of the eco or home in which all the living beings reside. The actions of killing of a seed or a grain for sustain of human body may not be regarded as a case of violence as no spirit of revenge or enmity stands. In the physical nature such urges for self sustain once procreate the equity in the world of existence.

In the *Dhammapada,* it has been rightly remarked by the Buddha that enmity should not be counteracted by enmity. Enmity is conquered by non enmity. It is an eternal law.

na hi vereṇa verāṇi sammantidha kadācana/
avereṇa ca sammanti esa dhammo sanatano//"

'di na nam yang khro ba yis
dgra rnams zhi bar mi byed kyang/
khro ba med pas zhi bar 'gyur/
'di ni gyung drung chos yin no/[7]

Violence is always provoked by enmity and contrarily non-violence is the negation of enmity. It shows the maturity of the mind (*citta*) which is attained by the practice of *shīla* (moral precepts), *samādhi* (mental concentration) and *prajñā* (wisdom).

A person should not be enemical to the nature under any circumstance. Because a human being is a part of the nature.

The Buddha attained his *bodhi* in the congenial surrounding and he taught his followers to be akin to the nature, so there would be no imbalance or bifurcation from the self nature (rang bzhin).

In the early phase of Buddhism when the monasteries were not built Shākyamuni instructed his disciples to accommodate themselves to the nature as best as they could. He prescribed the four *nishrayas*. Subsequently he taught them to practice *yoga* under the open sky secluded in sylvan area. Moreover the monasteries were built far away from the madding crowd of a city or human locality, or at the cave of a mountain inaccessible to the common public. All these facts help us to understand Gautama's idea of balance or equity between man and the nature. The Buddhist texts insist on keeping how to maintain a cordial relationship of human beings with the natural phenomena around them.

The verse of *Chos kyi tshigs su bcad pa (Dhammapada)* refers to this:

gang gis srog ni 'gum byed pa /
des na 'phags par mi 'gyur te /
srog chags kun la mi 'tshe ba
'phags pa zhes byar brjod pa yin /"[8]

By killing living beings one does not become an *Arya.* By non-killingness towards all living beings one is called an *Arya.*

It is observed that nonviolence as a coronary of nature awareness continues in the Buddhist literature. The Tibetan translations of the *Udānavarga* and the *Chos kyi tshigs su bcad pa* (Dhammapada) in Pali translated by Dge 'dun chos 'phel in our century reveal, the similarity.

"rtag tu gtsang ma 'tshol ba dang /
thub chod mi byed 'dzin bag can

'tsho ba dag la lta ba yi /
ngo tsha zhes pa'i 'tsho ba dka'a" /

"rtag tu gtsang ma 'tshol ba dang /
skyon med kha bsag med pa dang
dag pa'i 'tsho ba la ltos ba'i
ngo tsha can rnamas daka'a bar 'tsho."[9]

Hard is the life of a modest one who ever seeks purity, being detached, humble. He lives in purity and is intelligent. (Translated by Dge 'dun chos 'phel and George Roerich).

Notes & References

1. An instance of a Tibetan translation (yig sgyur) from the Pali version of the Dhammapada i.e. Khuddaka Nikāya by gedun choephel (gde' aun chos' phel and George N. Roerich, Mahabodhi Society, 1944).
2. Khaggavewana Sutta, *Sutta Nipāta,* Khuddaka Nikaya.
3. In Theravada, a self—enlightened being who contemplates dependent origination and attains realisation of truth without a teacher.
4. Dhammapada (Pali-Tibetan) papavagga, ed. by C.R. Lama . (Central Institute of Higher Tibetan Studies, Sarnath, Varanasi, 1982) Chapter-IX. Verse 10 p. 127.
5. *Ibid.,* attavagga XII. 9. p. 166.
6. "Sabbe papa piyauba subasaya dukkhạ—Pabhikula apiyavaha piyajivino, jiviukama sabhisim jiviyam piyam, esa bhaggo aritrahim paveiye jahettha kusale nobalimpijjasi", Acaranga 3/2.
7. Dhammapada, Yamaka Vagga I. 5. p 5.
8. *Ibid,* Dhammattha—Vagga XIX. 15. p 271.
9. No reference.

12

An Analysis of the Authentic Authorship of the Tibetan Medical Treatise "Cha lag bco brgyad" (12th century AD) and a Description of its Historical Background

Barbara Gerke

Introduction

The Gyushi (*rgyud bzhi;* known as "*The Four Medical Tantras*") are the most famous and fundamental works of all Tibetan medical literature. So pervasive is their influence that they have been in continuous use since the 12th century. This paper deals with a medical text on the Gyushi known as the *cha lag bco brgyad* (lit. "The Eighteen Implementations"). This text was of major importance for traditional Tibetan medical studies between the 12th and 16th century AD. Subsequent to this period, it basically disappeared from the medical curricula. Its authorship is generally attributed to the outstanding physician of the early 12th century, Yuthog Yontan Gonpo the Younger (*gyu thog yon tan mgon po gsar ma;* 1112-1203; hereafter referred to as Yuthog). This treatise should not be viewed and analysed apart from the vast corpus of Tibetan medical literature and its history. Rather it should be viewed in terms of its historical context. Studying the commentary in this way raises a number of interesting questions. Why did it enjoy such popularity for five hundred years and then suddenly disappeared into the abyss of heavy criticism? Who were its authors and how is the development of traditional medicine in Tibet at that time reflected in its compilation?

Part one of this paper concentrates on the medical history related to the work. Part two examines the eighteen texts and their diverse authorship.

The Lhasa edition of the 17th century version of the *cha lag bco brgyad* was reprinted by Lokesh Chandra in 1968.[1] Other private manuscript versions may be available from individual physicians scattered throughout the Himalayan region. An incomplete edition of the original block-print manuscript form the major part of the Tibetan medical manuscript collection at the Museum of the Asiatic Society, Calcutta.[2] Eleven out of the eighteen works are available at the museum. Seven of these are clearly mentioned as being authored by Yuthog. One could assume that the remaining xylographs found their origins in the same source. But further research shows that other historical works quote different authors, even for those texts of this collection mentioning Yuthog as author. Such divergence of opinion in authorship, and the historical background, are discussed in this paper. This debate lends further insight into the history of Tibetan medical literature that was moulded by its amalgamation with other medical cultures and nurtured by its own indigenous traditions.

Unfortunately, the date of publication is not mentioned in the xylographs stored at the Asiatic Society. They were all published, however, in *Ganden Puntsoling (dga' ldan phun tsogs gling)* which is one of the main Tibetan *Gelugpa (dge lugs pa)* monasteries. Situated 62 km north-east of Lhasa, it was founded in 1416 by Tsongkhapa *(gtzong kha pa)* the head of the Yellow or *Gelugpa* sect. It became one of the important block printing presses in Tibet along with others at Derge. Lhasa, Kumbum and Narthang. The technique of wood-block prints was introduced to Tibet from China only in the 15th century and was expensive, therefore hand written copies were much in use.

I
Historical Background

An Overview

In the history of Tibetan medicine there have been two eminent physicians holding the name of Yuthog Yontan Gonpo (*gyu thog yon tan mgon po)*. Yuthog Yontan Gonpo the Elder (708-833 AD) appeared during the early period of the introduction of Buddhism to Tibet (4th to 10th century). He was heading the "New Medical School" as one of the nine private court physicians (*rgyal po bla sman dgu)* of King Trisong Deutsen *(khri srong lde'u btzan;* 755-797). [3] At this time, scholars were occupied with the translation of medical works from neighbouring countries and with the task of accumulating knowledge. "The important point is not so much the fact that texts were translated but what these translations achieved by stimulating the minds of the people who were eager to absorb and assimilate new ideas." [4]

Not a single piece of original writing by Tibetan doctors can be authenticated from this period[5], in spite of the fact that the biography of Yuthog the Elder attributes countless works to him[6]. Most scholars believe that none of these works has survived. Exceptionally, Rechung Rinpoche (Rechung, 1973, p285) attributes text eight of the *cha la bco brgyad* to Yuthog the Elder, but this data differs from other sources.

Yuthog the Younger (1112-1203) was born into the latter period of Buddhist expansion in Tibet (10th century onwards).

His predecessor, Rinchen Zangpo *(rin chen bzang po;* 958-1055), gave new inspiration to the most influential medical school at the monastery of Tholing (*mtho lding*), in West Tibet. This school was established during the 8th century. Because of the geographical proximity to Western Tibet and the Centres of Higher Studies in North India, where Buddhism was still flourishing, Rinchen Zangpo concentrated on the translation and editing of Indian texts, in total 158, including medical treatises, such as Vagbhata's *Astangahridayasamhita.*

Presumably Vagbhata lived from 550 to 600 AD.[7] He revered the ancient Vedic precepts as well as Buddhist practices that were then popular in India. The *Astangahridayasamhita* is a systematised text of human illness and therapy in six sections (Skt. sthana) which incorporates the "Eight Branches", known as "*astangahridaya*" in Sanskrit and "yan lag brgyad pa" in Tibetan. *Astangahridayasamhita* earned priority among Indian Ayurvedic scholars and was included in The Great Triad (*Skt. brhat trayi)* of Ayurvedic literature. It reached Tibet via Nepal presumably in the 11th century AD.[8]

Yuthog the Younger established his own medical tradition, known as the Yuthog Nyingthig (gyu thog snying thig), in Central Tibet. This tradition demonstrates with originality a new independent direction of Oriental medicine in Tibet. Principal features of this school of thought include a vivid activity in compiling indigenous medical literature in relationship with Buddhist thought, relying on the various traditions that had entered Tibet by that time as well as the original school of Bon. The cha lag bco brgyad originated from this new school of Yuthog and his students.

YUTHOG YONTAN GONPO THE ELDER (708-833 AD)

Yuthog Yontan the Elder (*rnying ma*), born in the Earth-Male-Monkey year 708, was one of the most respected physicians in the Tibetan medical tradition and is said to have lived for 125 years. He was initiated into the medical wisdom by the translator Vairocana *(pha' bo*, also known as Berozana) who was one of the first Buddhist monks in Tibet, and a main disciple of Padmasambhava, the Indian tantric who introduced the tradition of Indian Mahayana Buddhism to Tibet during the 8th century.[9]

Vairocana transmitted the teachings of the *Gyushi* to Yuthog the Elder. The term *Gyushi* is an abbreviation for "*bdud rtzi snying po yan lag brgyad pa gsang ba man ngag gyi rgyud*". The title of this 156—chapter treatise, written in 5900 verses, may be translated as "The nectar essence of the eight branches of healing—a treatise of secret oral instruction".[10] Vairocana himself had obtained its knowledge from the Kashmiri Pandit Dawa Gaba (*zla ba dga' ba)* also known as Candrandana.[11]

The Concealment and Rediscovery of the *Gyushi*

The historian, Jaya Pandita Lobsang Thinle (blo bzang 'phrin las), born in Mongolia in 1642, well documented the history of Tibetan medicine. He wrote: "...during the reign of King Trisong Deutsen (*khri srong lde'u btzan;* 755-797), when medical scientists gathered from all areas and translated many medical works and commentaries ... the famous rgyud bzhi were considered the summit of medical science ...".[12]

Tradition says that the contemporary minds of those who would read the *Gyushi* were not yet ready to receive it. Therefore they were concealed as a "treasure" (*gter ma*) inside a pillar on the second floor of the main temple in the highest, five storied building in the centre of the monastery at Samye *(bsam yas)*.[13]

There is still controversy over as to who actually discovered them and should be considered as the 'Revealer' *(gter bston)*. Most publications mention a monk called Trapa Ngonshe *(grwa pa mngon shes;* 1012-1090) and date the rediscovery at 1038.[14] Besides this tradition, there are other

Terma discovery stories about the Gyushi. They generally mention Yuthog the Younger as being the 'Revealer' himself.[15]

On the Origin of the *Gyushi*

Some two hundred years later, the discussion among scholars about the origin of the *Gyushi*—whether it was primarily an Indian or Tibetan work—had become an important issue which was elaborately discussed and debated. In general, the Tibetan tradition considers this work as a translation of an Indian original, the Sanskrit title being "*Amrtahridaya-angaastaguhyaupadesatantra nama*". But to date, a Sanskrit version has not yet been discovered and the attempt to reconstruct the lost Sanskrit "original" from the Tibetan version does not prove its existence either.

Strangely enough the treatise was not included in the works of Buton Rinchendup (bu ston rin chen grub; 1290-1364) who carefully checked for authenticity the Sanskrit and Tibetan literature which was available to him in the 14th century, and compiled the Tibetan canon of Kanjur *(bka' 'gyur)* and Tanjur *(bstan 'gyur)*. He incorporated 22 medical treatises of Indian Ayurvedic origin in the Tanjur.[16] The *Gyushi,* being the main medical treatise even then, must have been known to him, since he had worked as a teacher at the *Sakya (sa skya)* monastery which was widely known as the 'Medical City' *(sman grong)* being the site of a college of Tibetan medicine.[17]

The content of these "Four Treatises", however, indeed shows an affinity to Indian medicine. Such Indian roots can be traced in the mythological history described in the first treatise *(rtsa ba'i rgyud)* or in the mentioning of foods that are neither found nor eaten in Tibet.[18] But also the entire physiology with its three basic principles Lung, Tipa and

Bakan *(rlung, mkhris pa, bad kan)* and the medical terminology, which to a great extent is confirm with Vagbhata's Ayurvedic treatise *Astangahridayasamhita*[19] prove a strong Indian influence on the work. On the other hand the *Gyushi* provides knowledge on pulse[20] and urine diagnosis based on the five elements and the fundamental principles of Chinese astrology, that is not to be found in contemporary Indian medical literature, and which therefore must have originated from other sources. Moreover, the tradition of indigenous healing arts that existed in Bon settlements in Gilgit, Guge and Purang within the Shang Shung *(zhang zhung)* also had its impact on the development of Tibetan medicine. In conclusion, one can assume that the present version of the *Gyushi* is based on Indian sources, mainly the *Astangahridayasamhita* by Vagbhata[21] and must have been considerably elaborated and re-edited by Yuthog under the influence of Chinese medical texts, such as the Somaraja *(Tib. zla ba'i rgyal po)*[22] and his own medical experiences based on indigenous Tibetan medical knowledge.

According to Desi Sangye Gyatso (1653-1705) Yuthog re-edited Vagbhata's text in conformity with Chinese ideas: "Yuthog Yontan Gonpo only added single parts to the incomplete paragraphs of the original text (rtza) of the rgyud bzhi, with the help of the text *zla ba'i rgyal po,* that was translated from Chinese, and others, for the purpose of concurring the quintessence (of the *rgyud bzhi)* with (the conditions of) Tibet. He added some parts to the bdud rtzi snying po yan lag brgyad pa *(bsang ba) mang ngag gi rgyud,* that is in the *phyi ma rgyud and man ngag rgyud* numerous supplements, in the *rtza rgyud* a number of chapters *(rgyud le'u grangs)* and in the *bshad brgyud* (some) supplementary chapters, etc., ..." [23]

The teaching of the *Gyushi* was transmitted from teacher to student over the centuries and the lineages are documented in various historical *thob yig (thob yig)*. A *thob yig* is a repertory, that tells the historical background, often hemming myths to facts, of the Tibetan culture. In the case of the thob yig by Jaya Pandita the medical history is described till the second half of the 18th century.[24]

The continuity of the teaching through a living lineage is one of the most remarkable features of the Tibetan culture and has survived till the present time. It is possible to study the existing ancient texts in each generation anew, but to keep a transmission, from teacher to disciple, by means of initiation and oral instructions, flowing, throughout possibly more than a hundred generations, over a period of more than a millennia, till the present time, is a cultural achievement that only very few cultures have been able to accomplish.

YUTHOG YONTAN GONPO THE YOUNGER (1112-1203)

Even though there is controversy about the 'Revealer' and the time of the rediscovery of the *Gyushi*, it is clear that this Terma reached the hands of Yuthog in the 12th century. Without going further into this discussion in the context of this paper, it is, however, interesting to note that even though the original version of the *Gyushi* from the 8th century was available to Yuthog the Younger in the 12th century, he felt the need to travel extensively and research medicine in India further. One account of the 16th century, the *mkhas pa'i dga' ston by Tsugla Tengwa (gtzug lag phreng ba)*, describes him overcoming great hardships with the help of the Indian medicine Goddess *(sman gyi bla mo)*. His accomplishment of the Indian sciences is said to have turned him into a leader of many Indian Pandits and Siddhas. At his age of 76 he disappeared in light without leaving any physical residues behind.[25]

The numerous vitae concerning Yuthog in the various thob yig describe him as an extremely gifted person. Like Jaya Pandita, Tsugla Tengwa also recounts the life story of

Yuthog with all of his miraculous healings and Siddha attainments. But as in most Tibetan historical writings, it is often impossible to distinguish between legend and historical facts.

Yuthog travelled through the high lands of Tibet to receive the oral instructions and explanations of respected teachers such as Dardag from Central Tibet *(dbus pa dar grags)*. Furthermore, commentaries like the *rgyud 'di gzung 'grel man ngag dang bshad pa* were already available to Yuthog before his age of 18. Therefore one can assume that he must have had quite an extensive knowledge of what was known as Tibetan medicine at that time, when he first journeyed to India. [26]

The *Gyushi* is written in poetic form and often in a secret language not decipherable without a commentary or oral explanation from an experienced teacher. Was the content of the Gyushi still incomprehensible to Yuthog or was his desire for medical knowledge simply not satisfied by it? In the 8th century, Yuthog the Elder in his prophecies foresaw that the younger Yuthog would have to journey to India because the lineage of the quintessence of preparing the medicines *(bdud rtzi sman grub)* would be corrupted and would need to be reformed through new instructions by the "16 Goddesses of Medicine" in India. [27]

Of royal descent, born in Central Tibet in the Fire-Male-Horse year 1112, Yuthog journeyed to India six times and was to follow his quest of discovering traditional Indian medical knowledge. Through him, medical science in Tibet was again enriched and revived by the infusion of contemporary Indian practices of healing. Historically, his journeys took place at an important time as, shortly afterwards, the Islamic conquest was to destroy the flourishing culture of Buddhism and, along with it, most of its extensive literature of medicine and other sciences, especially that of Northern

India. Thus Yuthog contributed enormously to the survival of medical knowledge of Indian origin on the isolated plateau of Tibet.

Yuthog's Version of the *Gyushi*

The Kalachakra Tantra reached Tibet in 1027. Vagbhata's *Astangahridayasamhita* was to be translated into Tibetan in the same century. Yuthog also was affiliated with the medical lineage of Atisha who came to Tibet in 1042 and taught the "Eight branches of Healing" (yan lag brgyad pa) to Tibetan physicians from *Nethang (sne thang).*[28] All these scriptures reached Yuthog, and he included their knowledge in his own writings.

An important and interesting question which is also yet to be addressed is how the original version of the Gyushi was re-formulated by Yuthog and to what extent—sources other than Indian-Chinese, Persian and a lot of native Tibetan based on the old Bon tradition and other folk traditions of Tibet were included.

Re-discovery of Yuthog's Version of the Gyushi in the 16th century

Yuthog prepared a hand-written version of his new edition of the *Gyushi.* He then placed it in hiding and it was rediscovered only in 1542 by the reputed physician Zurkha Lodo Gyalpo (*zur mkhar blo gros rgyal po*, 1509-1579). During this time the medical teachings had gone through a period of decline and had suffered from too many corrupt interpolations. Of course, 'rediscovery' implies 're-interpretation' as well as continuity.[29] Lodo Gyalpo published this authentic revised edition and thus made an important contribution to the continuity of Yuthog's lineage in Tibetan medicine.[30]

The Lineage continues

Yuthog's lineage, which combines medical practice with spiritual instructions and esoteric insight, survived. In 1696, the Chakpori Medical College, also known as Menpa Datsan *(sman pa gra tsang)*, was founded on one of the Lhasa hills, facing the Potala from where, the Vth Dalai Lama, Ngawang Lobsang Gyatso *(ngag dbang blo bzang rgya mtso;* 1617-1682) had initiated its establishment before his death through his regent Sangye Gyatso (1653-1705). The college uniquely integrated medical practice with Buddhist teaching. Here, Yuthog's lineage was kept alive by the monastic medical practitioners.

After 1959, when Menpa Datsan fell into ruins, along with some of the few last masters of Tibetan medicine the lineage entered India, where Yuthog had received his initiations about 750 years ago. Some of the lineage holders have made the attempt to gather students and disciples, and have settled in the Himalayan region and even crossed the borders into the Western countries. History surprises.

II
The *cha lag bco brgyad*

Yuthog presented his discoveries in various medical writings. Of these, the *cha lag bco brgyad* (lit. "The Eighteen Implementations") became the most famous. A compilation of 18 independent medical text, they touch upon numerous subjects of Tibetan medicine. This work was of major importance to medical studies till the middle of the 17th century, especially among the physicians of *Dangti (brang ti) and Zurlug (zur lugs)* [31], two of the schools of Tibetan medicine.

Controversial Authorship of Yuthog's Writings

Sources of analysis

In Tibet it was customary among students to pay homage to their teachers *(bla ma)* by attributing to them the authorship of their compositions. And curiously enough, teachers prepared books in the students' names as well. Modern day researchers, therefore, face difficulties in verifying the authenticity of authors and their xylographs.

The authorship of the *cha lag bco brgyad* is not entirely attributable to Yuthog as it is generally said; certain chapters were written by his students and others, apparently, were translated from Chinese sources. In order to come to a clearer view the following works were consulted:

Two Versions of the *cha lag bco brgyad* (17th century)

The colophons of the 17th century Lhasa edition of cha lag bco brgyad, reprinted in "Yuthog's treatise on Tibetan Medicine", edited by Lokesh Chandra. Satapitaka Series Vol. 72. New Delhi 1968. (abbr. LC)

Date of publication not mentioned:

The colophons of the eleven available manuscripts of the *cha lag bco brgyad* (including the index) in the collection of non-canonical Tibetan medical manuscripts at the Asiatic Society, Calcutta. The manuscripts that comprise texts of the *cha lag bco brgyad* are: ST 109 (= index), ST 110 (= text 1), ST 112 (= text 4), ST 113(= text 3), ST 114 (= text 10), ST 115 (= text 11), ST 116+ ST 123 (= text 13), ST 117 (= text 7), ST 118 (= text18), ST 120 (= text 15), ST 121 (= text 17). (abbr. AS)

Historical Works

16th century:

The *mkhas pa'i dga' ston*[32] by Tsugla Tengwa *(gtzug lag phreng ba;* 1504-1566), also known as Chogyal Dondub *(chos rgyal don grub)*. The composition of the work started in 1545. The chapter on medical history was completed in 1563/1564. Even though this work is not as detailed as Jaya Pandita's *thob yig,* it is of interest because it was compiled about 140 years earlier. (abbr. TT) [33]

Late 17th/early 18th century:

The repetitorium *chos kyi thob yig gsal ba'i me long* by Jaya Pandita Lobsang Thinle *(blo bzang 'phrin las)* also known as Shakya Tsunpa Lobsang Thinle *(shakya'i btzun pa blo bzang 'phrin las),* who was born in 1642 in Mongolia. The *thob yig* was completed in 1702. Beijing Block Print. Four Volumes, 298+316+320+304 folios. The chapter on medicine is in the 2nd saga, I/77-108. (abbr. JP). The treatise was translated into German by Manfred Taube.[34]

Both works agree in their comments on the authorship of the *cha lag bco brgyad.* Jaya Pandita's list of authors refers most probably to an older work, dated approximately 140 years earlier. But it is certain that Jaya Pandita did not merely copy the information from *mkhas pa'i dga' ston,* as much of his data is not available in Tsugla Tengwa's work. [35]

Commentary on the Gyushi

17th Century:

Desi Sangye Gyatso's *(sde srid sangs rgyas rgya mtso;* 1653-1705) "Blue Lapis lazuli" *(vaidurya sngon po*[36]; completed in 1687-1688). This text presents a formidable critique of the *cha lag bco brgyad* which caused a drastic decline in its popularity. (abbr. SG)

Additional Sources

In an effort to relieve any further doubts on the question of authorship, at times supplementary information is taken from two additional sources:

18th century:

Klongdol Lama Nawang Lobsang *(klong rdol bla ma ngag dbang blo bzang;* born in 1719) and his *gsung 'bum.* (Beijing block print. folio 42-72). The chapters on medicine are presented in the works entitled *ming gi grangs*, Vol. ma folio 11-13. (abbr. KL)

19th century:

Akhu Rinpoche Sherab Gyatso *(a khu rin po che shes rab rgya mtso;* 1803-1857): *dpe rgyun dkon pa 'ga' zhig gi tho yig don gnyer kyi kunda bzhad pa'i zla 'od 'bum gyi snye ma.*—edited by Lokesh Chandra 1963, iii, 503-601. In chapter 20 *(gso ba rig pa'i khor)* 297 titles of Tibetan medical works are mentioned. (LC 13 073-13 369). The author was a student of the Vth Dalai Lama and a teacher of Jaya Pandita. He is said to have been the reincarnation of Klongdol Lama the famous scholar of the 18th century, introduced above.[37] (abbr. AR)

The Group of Authors

Before presenting the 18 texts, it is important to look at Yuthog's disciples who often are mentioned as authors of some of the 18 implementations. Tradition has it that Yuthog was surrounded by students "as numerous as the sand corns on this earth"[38]. More important in verifying his importance as a medical scholar than this metaphor, characteristically Tibetan, are those students that have been mentioned by name. In Yuthog's biography by Tsugla Tengwa, the most important students of the famous physician are: Jangman Lebbe *(ljang sman sleb be),* Balman Nyimapal *('bal sman nyi ma spal),* Ja Yeshezung *(rja ye shes gzungs)*, Tonpa Atse *(ston pa a tzes)*[39], Shagram Nyimapal *(gshag ram nyi ma dpal),* Yuthog Soseng *(gyu thog bsod seng),* Sumton Yeshezung *(sum ston ye shes gzungs)* and Getse Rogchung *(dge brtze rog chung).*[40] In-comparison, 140 years later, Jaya Pandita states: "Among his most important students the first is Sumton Yeshezung *(sum ston ye shes gzungs)*; others were Jangman Lebbe *(ljang sman sleb be)*, Balman Nyimapal *('bal sman nyi ma dpal)*, Tonpa Athse *(ston pa a tses)*, Sharam Nyimapal *(shag ram pa nyi ma dpal)*, Yuthog Sonam Senge *(gyu thog bsod nams seng ge)* and Geshe Rogchung *(dge bshes rog chung)*.[41]

YUTHOG'S STUDENTS SUMTÖN YESHEZUNG AND JA YESHEZUNG

Among all these students, Sumton Yeshezung and Ja Yeshezung deserve the most attention. It is not really clear whether this two names refer to the same person as at times they are both mentioned in the same list. Sumton Yeshezung wrote the index *(dkar chag)* of the cha lag bco brgyad and both students appear as author or co-author of several of its works. Sumton Yeshezung independently composed a number of treatises on Tibetan medicine.[42] It seems that his importance was only realised more than a century after the publication of the *mkhas pa'i dga' ston,* because Tsugla Tengwa, at the end of the 16th century, mentions Sumton Yeshezung only as the seventh in the list of Yuthog's students.

In comparison, Jaya Pandita, in the early 18th century, places him first in the list and refers to him quite often in his *thob yig*.[43] The reason for this elevation in status could be some form of special recognition that he received from the monastic and political community around the Vth Dalai Lama and Desi Sangye Gyatso. Surprisingly, Ja Yeshezung is always mentioned first by both historians in the enumeration of Yuthog's students. Which of them deserves the honour of being attributed the authorship for the five works (text 3, 4, 5, 6, 8) is unclear as both of them appear in the lists.

Sumton Yeshezung's main student was Gyimchog Tshoje Zhonu Yeshe *(gyim phyogs 'tsho byed gzhon nu ye shes)* who, in LC's edition of the *cha lag bco brgyad,* is mentioned as the author of part 1.2 of text twelve. This clearly indicates that the texts of the *cha lag bco brgyad* were written over at least two generations. Looking further we find that in one colophon JP mentions the physician of Dangti, Palden Gyaltsen *(brang ti dpal ldan rgyal mtsan)*, as the author of text four. The colophon reads: "This commentary was requested by Yuthog Menpa Geshe Manju *(gyu thog sman pa dge shes manju)* from the physician of Dangti, Palden Gyalsten *(dpal ldan rgyal mtsan)*."[44] This reference, of course, could also mean that Palden Gyaltsen only continued the tradition of this text.[45] However, this physician is mentioned by JP in the 7th generation after Sumton Yeshezung. This would date his writings at least a hundred years later.[46] The fourth text might, therefore, have been added to the collection much later.

THE 18 TEXTS OF THE *cha lag bco brgyad*

In the following the 18 texts are introduced with their title and their authors (for a summary see the table (pp. 110-111).Differences in spellings of titles in different versions are added in brackets.

Text 1:

Title: *khog dbug ('bubs) khyung chen lding ba*

Author: Yuthog, as also stated in AS and LC, but according to JP (I/91) they were written by a Bonpo or Nyingma physician and according to TT (49) they were authored by Yeshezung or one of Yuthog's students. TT comments on this text: "...its phrases *(tha snyad)* are not inspiring and imitate other's opinion..." (TT, 49). Sangye Gyatso calls this work "an epigone", that is, a piece which is directly quoted from a book *(dpe blangs pa)*, in this case, a book of Chinese divination (IV/224/2).

Text 2:

Title: *stong thun mdzes pa'i 'ja' ris*

Author: Yuthog, as also stated in LC, but according to JP (I/91) they were written by a Bonpo or Nyingma physician and according to TT they were authored by Ja Yeshezung or one of Yuthog's students. This text is missing in the AS collection. TT comments also on this text: "...its phrases *(tha snyad)* are not inspiring and imitate other's opinion..." (TT, 49). Sangye Gyatso calls this work also "an epigone of Chinese divination".

Text 3:

Title: *sa dpyad (bcad) stag mo'i rngam thabs*

Author: no author is mentioned in LC. AS attributes the authorship to Yuthog himself, but JP claims the actual authors were four of Yuthog's students, i.e. Ja Yeshezung, Shagrampa Nyimapal, Balsam Nyimapal and Sumton Yeshezung (JP I/91). No details are available from TT. Sangye Gyatso calls also this work an epigone (see text 1 and 2).

Text 4:

Title: *tika mun sel sgron me*

Author: No author is mentioned in LC. TT attributes the authorship to Ja Yeshezung or other disciples of Yuthog (TT, 49), and JP states that the text was written by the four students Ja Yeshezung, Shagrampa Nyimapal, Balsam Nyimapal and Sumton Yeshezung (JP I/91). As mentioned in the AS collection, Yuthog himself was the author. But Desi Sangye Gyatso denies Yuthog's or Sumton's authorship for this text. According to him, it was written by a "Non-Buddhist" *(ma das pa zhig gis byas)* and "apart from a few therapeutic advises does not further the understanding of the Gyushi"(IV/224/2).

Text 5:

Title: *'grel ba 'bum chung gsal sgron nor bu'i 'phreng mdzes*

Author: According to the colophon in LC, the author was Yuthog's student Jnanadhara *(= ye shes gsungs)*. This statement is supported by Akhu Rinpoche's work (LC, 1963, 13 25). TT mentions Ja Yeshezung or another disciple of Yuthog (TT/49) as the author. JP states that the text was written by the four students, Ja Yeshezung, Shagrampa Nyimapal, Balsam Nyimapal and Sumton Yeshezung (JP I/ 91). He also claims that the text was corrected some time later *(dus phyis)* by the scholar Paljor (mkhas pa dpal 'byor). Like text four, Desi Sangye Gyatso states that neither Yuthog nor Sumton wrote this text but, on the contrary, says that it was written by a "Non-Buddhist" (ma das pa zhig gis byas). "Apart from a few therapeutic advises," he says, the work "does not further the understanding of the *Gyushi*" (IV/224/2). This text is not available in the AS collection.

Text 6:

Title: *rtzod bzlog gegs sel 'khor lo*

Author: According to LC, this work was compiled by Yuthog's teacher Konkyab *('tso byed dkon skyabs)*. AS mentions Yuthog, and according to JP, the text was compiled by Yuthog's students, Ja Yeshezung, Shagrampa Nyimapal, Balsam Nyimapal and Sumton Yeshezung (JP I/91). TT also mentions Ja Yeshezung and others. As for text four and five, Desi Sangye Gyatso denies their authorship for this work and launches the same criticism (already mentioned above.)

Text 7:

Title: *skor tsoms stong thun bcu gcig*

Author: In the AS collection, no author is mentioned. Three other sources, however, TT and JP and LC, attribute this work to Yuthog.

Text 8:

Title: *ming don brda sprod rnam lnga* (a medical glossary)

Author: LC mentions a scholar named Vairocana, JP ascribes the authorship to Ja Yeshezung, Shagrampa Nyimapal, Balsam Nyimapal and Sumton Yeshezung (JP I/ 91), in accordance with TT. This work is not available in the AS collection. Text eight is the only work of this collection, which one source (Rechung, 1973, p285) attributes to Yuthog the Elder.

Text 9:

Title: rin chen spungs pa'i mdzes rgyan

Author: TT and JP, both mention Yuthog. No author is mentioned by LC and the text is not available in the AS collection.

Text 10:

Title: *kha 'thor rin cen phung po*

Author: The manuscript colophon at the AS reads: "from the oral lineage heard by the Sages", which might mean Yuthog and his lineage. TT and JP ascribe the authorship, on which there is no data in LC, to Yuthog.

Text 11:

Title: *lag len dmar khrid yig chung*

Author: All sources agree that the author of this work is Yuthog.

Text 12: This work is divided into three parts. TT and JP attribute the general authorship to Yuthog, the text is missing in the AS collection, only the colophons in LC give further details:

1. *Title: brgyud pa'i rnam thar med thabs med pa*

Author: The first part is attributed to Yeshezung *(ye shes gsungs)*. The second part, which is larger than the others completely differs in content and style. Its lyrical rhythm was added somewhat later by Tshoje Shonu Yeshe *('tso byed gzhon nu ye shes)*, a student of Yeshezung.

2. Title: *rtza'i spra sgrub med thabs med pa*

Author: This text is of Chinese origin, and was translated by Vairocana. The colophon also mentions a Trapa Ngonshe *(grva pa mngon shes)*

3. Title: *sri'u gso ba med thabs med pa*

Author: of Chinese origin, translated by Vairocana.

Text 13:

Title: *yang sbabs gab pa bco brgyad*

Author: This is the second work of the collection where Yuthog is mentioned by all sources as the author.

Text 14:

Title: *khyad par zab pa rnam gsum*

Author: This text is not available in the AS collection. There is no data in LC, but TT and JP mention Yuthog as author.

Text 15:

Title: *mkhas khyad ngo mtsar bzhi sbrugs (sprugs)*

Author: The colophons of AS and LC do not mention any author. TT and JP, both ascribe the authorship to Yuthog.

Text 16:

Title: *rgyud chung bdud rtzi snying po*

Author: This text is not available at the AS. TT mentions Yuthog as author. So does JP. LC mentions Dawa Ngonga *(zla ba mngon dga')*. Desi Sangye Gyatso comments that this text is hardly of any use for a deeper understanding of the 'Oral Instruction Tantra' *(man ngag gyi rgyud)*, the third part of the Gyushi.(IV/224/ 2)

Text 17:

Title: *gso dpyad mu tig 'phreng ba*

Author: All sources mention Yuthog as author. But Desi Sangye Gyatso comments that it is not a useful text (see text 16).

Text 18:

Title: *phan byed (bya) sngags 'bum dkar po*

Author: According to LC, this work is of Chinese origin and was translated by Vairocana. It is not available in the AS collection and is also not mentioned in the passages on the cha lag bco brgyad by TT and JP.

The data regarding the authorship of the *cha lag bco brgyad* are summarised in the following table.

Table I: The 18 texts of the *cha lag bco brgyad* and their authorship derived from four different sources:

Abbreviations:

N.M. = not mentioned; N/A. = text not available

Yuthog's students = Ja Yeshezung, Shagrampa Nyimapal, Balsam Nyimapal and Sumton Yeshezung

Yuthog's teacher = Konkyab ('tso byed dkon skyabs)

Table I

18 Texts	AS ?	TT 16th cent.	JP 17th cent.	LC 17th cent.
1.	Yuthog	Yuthog's students	a Bonpo or Nyingma physician	Yuthog
2	N/A	Yuthog's students	a Bonpo or Nyingma physician	Yuthog
3.	Yuthog	N.M.	Yuthog's students	N.M.
4.	Yuthog	Yuthog's students	Yuthog's students	N.M.
5.	N/A	Yuthog's students	Yuthog's students	Yeshezung

(Contd.)

18 Texts	AS ?	TT 16th cent.	JP 17th cent.	LC 17th cent.
6.	Yuthog	Yuthog's students	Yuthog's students	Yuthog's teacher
7.	N.M.	Yuthog	Yuthog	Yuthog
8.	N/A (acc. to Rechung) Yuthog the Elder	Yuthog's students	Yuthog's students	Vairocana
9.	N/A	Yuthog	Yuthog	N.M.
10.	Colophon: "from the oral lineage heard by the sages"	Yuthog	Yuthog	N.M.
11.	Yuthog	Yuthog	Yuthog	Yuthog
12.	N/A	Part I-III: Yuthog	Part I-III: Yuthog	Part I: 1. Students 2. Tsoje shonu Yeshe Part II: Chinese Part III: Chinese
13.	Yuthog	Yuthog	Yuthog	Yuthog
14.	N/A	Yuthog	Yuthog	N.M.
15.	N/M.	Yuthog	Yuthog	N.M.
16.	N/A	Yuthog	Yuthog	Dawa Ngona
17.	Yuthog	Yuthog	Yuthog	Yuthog
18.	N/A	N.M.	N.M.	Chinese

Desi Sangye Gyatso's Criticism on the *cha lag bco brgyad*

During the reign of the Vth Dalai Lama, the Regent Sangye Gyatso (1653-1705) who was also a physician and author, compiled a new and detailed commentary on the *Gyushi,* known as 'Blue Lapis lazuli' or *vaidurya sngon po.*[47] In this commentary, he criticised the cha lag bco brgyad. His comments have been included here, as they had a major impact on the popularity of the cha lag bco brgyad. The whole paragraph reads:[48]

"This cha lag bco brgyad is generally viewed as the most important (work) among the explanations and additions (of the *rgyud bzhi*). This view however does not withstand close inspection. The 16th text and the 17th text, are not really necessary for the understanding (*mkho ba chung ba*) of the man ngag rgyud [the third of the four treatises], of which they explain the content. The 1st and 2nd texts and the third text are only plagiarisms *(dpe blangs pa)* from Chinese divination. The 4th, 5th and 6th texts are most certainly not from the Elder or Younger Yuthog, or from Vairocana or Sumton [= Sumton Yeshezung] but from a non-Buddhist *(ma dad pa zhig gis byas)*; their content—apart from giving some advice for therapy—does not help in understanding the *rgyud bzhi*".[49]

How legitimate this criticism is, only a closer research of the content will reveal. Sangye Gyatso's work has been the main commentary used in Tibetan medical studies from its completion in 1687-1688, right through to the present day. His criticism of the cha lag bco brgyad had such an impact on other contemporaneous writers that various historical accounts written around the end of the 18th century, such the *gsung 'bum*, do not even mention Yuthog's treatise among the medical literature. Jaya Pandita's *thob yig*, on the other hand, written at the beginning of the 18th century, shortly after the publication of the 'Blue Lapis lazuli', still mentions it next to the *Gyushi* as the main medical work of the time.[50]

Conclusion

The divergences of opinion about the authorship suggest that there must have been various editions of the *cha lag bco brgyad* circulating among physicians in Tibet. The authorship cannot be traced with certainty for all works. Based on all sources consulted for this paper, only three of the 18 texts (text 11, 13 and 17) are with certainty attributable to Yuthog.

Text 7 must also have derived from Yuthog, with three out of four sources mentioning him.

As far as texts 9, 10, 14, and 15 are concerned, no controversy occurs over the authenticity of Yuthog in the data available, though the sources are incomplete. Most probably these works are from Yuthog as well, which comes to a collection of eight authentic works. Text 3, 4, 5, 6 and 8 seem to have originated from Yuthog's students or other physicians related to the lineage, but were added to the collection later. In sum, there are 13 of these. It is interesting that in the 19th century, Akhu Rinpoche included this treatise in his bibliography under the name of "13 or 18 Implementations" *(cha lag bcu gsum mam bco brgyad)*.[51] It appears that the authorship of texts 1, 2 and 16 was given, perhaps in honour, to Yuthog, much later. There seems to be a certain Chinese influence in text 12 and 18. Most likely, the collection was started by Yuthog and edited, compiled and elaborated upon by his students over a period of another two hundred years.

The interpolations which were infused into Yuthog's original version of his cha lag bco brgyad are a good example of what happened to many of the medical treatises in Tibet. Because of hand-written copies, which were prepared until the 15th century and even later, scribes could easily change, delete or add paragraphs to original writings. This habit gave space for personal interpretations and percolation. Known as textual gloss, these additional interpretations have led to colourful amalgamations. With the passage of time, subsequent researchers had to face a very difficult challenge to detect the primary sources. Also, a habit of not mentioning the actual author but of mistaking dedication to one's teacher or student for authorship led to confusion among researchers.

In Tibet, the active exchange of knowledge with India had stopped by the end of the 12th century. The inter-cultural influences of the Chinese, Greek, Persian and Indian traditions which were incorporated into the indigenous medical traditions of Tibet date back to the 12th century AD or before. Many of such treatises went through a gradual transformation of both content and language, during the centuries of the development of the enormous corpus of Tibetan medical literature. Most of this vast literature has yet to be researched.

NOTES

Part I

1. *Gyu thog yon tan mgon po:* YUTHOG's treatise on Tibetan Medicine. edited by LOKESH CHANDRA. Satapitaka Series Vol. 72. New Delhi 1968.
2. The collection of non-canonical Tibetan medical manuscripts at the Asiatic Society, Calcutta, are to be found under ST 109 to 123.
3. THINLE JAMPA. *gangs ldzong gso rig bstan pa'i nyin byed rim byon gyi rnam thar phyogs bsrigs zhes bya ba.* Tibetan Medical Institute, Dharamsala 1991, p. 34.
4. GUENTHER, HERBERT V. Foreword to Dargyay, Eva. M. *The Rise of Esoteric Buddhism in Tibet.* New York and Delhi 1977, 1978.
5. BOLSOKHOEVA, NATALIA D., *Introduction to the Studies of Tibetan Medical Sources.* Mandala Book Point. Kathmandu 1993. p. 11.
6. JAMPEL KUNZANG, RECHUNG RINPOCHE. *Tibetan Medicine, illustrated in original texts, presented and translated.* Berkeley and Los Angeles 1973; also: Publications of the Wellcome Institute of the History of Medicine, New Series Vol. XXIV. London 1973. (referred to here p. 312.)
7. MURTHY, K. R. SRIKANTHA. *Vagbhata's Astanga Hrdayam.* English & Sanskrit. Krishnadas Ayurveda Series 27, Vol. 1, Varanasi, 1991, 1995, 1997.
8. For details see: PATHAK, S.K.; TENZIN, S.; GERKE, B. Vagbhata's *Astanga Hrdaya Samhita and its importance to Indo-Tibetan Medical Studies.* in *AyurVijnana* Vol. III. Kalimpong 1997.
9. KARMAY SAMTEN G. "Vairocana and the *rgyud-bzhi*". in Tibetan Medicine. Series No. 12. Dharamsala 1989. p. 19.
10. Several versions of a literal translation of the title have been

published, for example: "The Ambrosia Heart Tantra". DONDEN, YESHI. Dharamsala 1977; or "Tantra of Secret Instructions on the Eight Branches, the Essence of the Elixir of Immortality". MEYER, FERNAND. *Introduction in Tibetan Medical Paintings.* London 1992; or "The Secret Quintessential Instructions on the Eight Branches of the Ambrosia Essence Tantra" in *Fundamentals of Tibetan Medicine*. Dharamsala 1995; or "The Quintessence Tantra: The Secret Oral Instruction of the Eight Branches of the Science of Healing" in CLARK, BARRY, *The Quintessence Tantras of Tibetan Medicine.* Snow Lion Publications. Ithaca, New York 1995.

11. KARMAY, SAMTEN G. *op. cit.* p. 28. and EMMERICK, RONALD E. "Sources of the *rgyud bzhi*". *Zeitschrift der Deutschen Morgenländischen Gesellschaft.* Supl. III, 2 (1977) pp. 1136.

12. JAYA PANDITA LOBSANG THINLE (*blo bzang 'phrin las*) *chos kyi thob yig gsal ba'i me long.* completed in 1702. Beijing Block Print. Four Volumes 298+316+320+304 folios. The chapter on medicine is in the 2nd *saga,* on folio I/77v-108v. The given quotation is on folio 82. Compare TAUBE, MANFRED. "Beiträge zur Geschichte der medizinischen Literatur Tibets" (Contributions to the History of Tibetan medical literature). Sankt Augustin 1981. p. 5, note 2.

13. According to JAYA PANDITA (likewise SANGYE GYATSO. *vai sngon.* Beijing block print, IV/213v4 and RECHUNG, London 1973, p. 17.) the text was concealed by PADMASAMBHAVA, but according to KLONGDOL LAMA (*klong rdol bla ma ngag dbang blo bzang*) in his *gsung 'bum.* (Beijing block print. folio 42-72. The chapters on medicine are in the works entitled *ming gi grangs*, Vol. ma folio 11-13. Here see ma 11v.) this was done by Yuthog the Elder, and according to the *cha lag bco brgyad* (ed. LOKESH CHANDRA. 1968, p. 331) by TRISONG DEUTSEN *(khri srong lde'u btzan*) and BAIROCANA (*bai ro tza na*). (Compare Taube, 1982, p. 27, note 118.)

14. KARMAY. op.cit. and DARGYAY. op.cit. p. 97. According to the calculation of KONGTRUL YONTAN GYATSO (*kong sprul yon tan rgya mtso;* 1813-1899) in his work *gter ston brga rtza'i rnam thar* the discovery took place in 1098.

15. KARMAY., *op.cit.* p. 20.

16. Listed by DAS, BHAGWAN. *Tibetan Medicine*. Delhi 1985. pp9.

17. TAUBE. *op.cit.* p. 53.

18. For example UNKRIG, WILHELM in FILCHNER, WILHELM. *Das Kloster Kumbum in Tibet.* Ein Beitrag zu seiner Geschichte. Berlin 1906. pp. 30 and 90-92.

19. So already OBERMILLER, EVGENY EVGENOVICH. Puti izucheniya tibetskoj medicinskoj literatury. In: *Bibliografija Vostoka* 8-9 (1935), Moscow 1936. pp. 48-60. And its English translation by HARRISH C. GUPTA: "Ways of Studying Tibetan Medical Literature", in *Tibetan Medicine,* Series No 12, LTWA. Dharamsala 1989. p. 9.

20. The teaching of pulse is missing in CARAKA, SUSHRUTA and VAGBHATA. TAUBE. *op.cit.* p. 26. note 112.

21. The relationship between VAGBHATA and *rgyud bzhi* are dealt with in detail by EMMERICK, R.E. (1977, pp. 1136-1141) according to which the Tibetan translation of *Astanga Hrdaya Samhita* forms a basis of the *rgyud bzhi.*. Compare TAUBE, M. *op.cit.* p. 26. note 111. For the English translation see: MURTHY, K. R. Srikantha. *Vagbhata's Astanga Hrdayam.* English & Sanskrit. Krishnadas Ayurveda Series 27, Vol. 1-3, Varanasi, 1991, 1995, 1997.

22. *sman dpyad zla ba'i rgyal po.* reprint: Dharamsala 1994. According to the colophon (1994 edition) the text was translated into Tibetan during the time of KING TRISONG DEUTSEN *(khri srong lde'u btzan,* 755-797) by HASHANG MAHAYANA (*ha shang ma ha ya na*) and BEROZANA (*bai ro tza na*). reprinted by the Tibetan Medical and Astro Institute, Dharamsala 1994.

23. SANGYE GYATSO. *op.cit.* IV/215.4-216.3 (compare TAUBE. 1982. p. 32)

24. JAYA PANDITA. *op.cit.* I/82.

25. TSUGLA TENGWA (*gtzug lag phreng ba*). Full title: *dam pa'i chos kyi 'khor los bsgyur ba rnams kyi dar ba gsal bar byed pa mkhas pa'i dga' ston zhes bya ba'i legs par bshad pa.* Another short title for the same work is: *lho brag chos 'byung.* The work was reprinted by LOKESH CHANDRA, New Delhi 1961. In this edition an exposé on the history of medicine is to be found in chapter five, under the sub-heading: *spyir rig gnas*

ji ltar byung tsul, folio 44-50, as well as in chapter 17 of the work. Here is referred to folio 47.

26 TAUBE. *op.cit.* p. 45.

27. RECHUNG. *op.cit.* p. 316.

28. TAUBE. *op.cit.* p. 44.

29. GUENTHER, HERBERT V. *op.cit.* p. iv.

30. THINLE, JAMPA. *gso rig bnyan pa'i nyen bye bzhugs.* Lhasa 1991. pp. 218-220.

Part-II

31. TAUBE. *op.cit.* p. 42.

32. TSUGLA TENGWA. *op.cit.*

33. As this manuscript is not available to the author, she relied on its excerpt German translations by Manfred Taube. TAUBE. op.cit.

34. TAUBE. *op.cit.*

35. TAUBE. *op.cit.* p41.

36. Full title: *gso ba rig pa'i bstan bchos sman bla'i dgongs rgyan rgyud bzhi gsal byed bai dur sngon po ma lli ka.* Beijing Block Print. folio 479-482. reprint: Lhasa. 1984.

37. TAUBE. *op.cit.* p. 9.

38. TT, *op.cit.* folio 49. and TAUBE. *op.cit.* p. 44.

39. in JP: *ston pa a tses.* The *cha lag bco brgyad* mentions him as a student of YUTHOG's midlife (LC, op.cit. pp. 332.)

40. The *cha lag bco brgyad* mentions him as a student of YUTHOG's later life. Compare TAUBE. *op.cit.* p. 45, note 189.

41. P. *op.cit.* folio 89. At another place (I/91) JP also mentions JA YESHEZUNG *(rja ye shes gzungs).*

42. listed by AKHU RINPOCHE, see LC 1961, *op.cit.* No. LC 13 123-13 126.

43. JP. *op.cit.* I/88, 90, 91, 100. compare TAUBE. *op.cit.* p. 48.

44. JP. *op.cit.* I/99.

45. TAUBE. *op.cit.* p. 42.

46. JP. *op.cit.* I/100.

47. Sangye Gyatso. *op.cit.*
48. Compare Taube, *op.cit.* p. 42.
49. Taube. *op.cit.* p. 42.
50. Taube. *op.cit.* p. 42.
51. AK. *op. cit.* in LC 1961, No. LC 13 106.

Tibetan Language and the Council in Standardization

13

Jampel Kalden

It is generally accepted that Tibet had no written language prior to the famous king Strong bTsan sGampo. The 33rd King sent Thonmi alongwith other sixteen companions to India to learn Sanskrit Language and Indian scripts. Except Thonmi others could not survive because of the hot climate and other factors. Thonmi learnt the Sanskrit language and the literature. He became a great scholar and thus he was named as Sambhota or Noble Tibetan. After returning to Tibet he invented the Tibetan scripts, modelling it from the *Brahmi* script of Gupta period. He also wrote eight Tibetan grammar aphorisms or Mulas which is known as *tsa-va* in Tibetan. Many translation work being carried on usually engaging two persons—one Indian Pandit and the other, a Tibetan Lo-Tsa-va, the translator. However, the translation work of Sanskrit literature into Tibetan language has been undertaken in real earnest during the King Thri-Song Dev-tsan in the second half of the 8th century. During his period, many scholars were invited from India and with a council of learnt Pandits and Lotsavas made a definite rules for translation work. The King Tri Ralpa Chen formed a council of Tibetan translators and commissioned them to compile the famous Tibetan-Sanskrit Dictionary known as bye-brag tu rtogs-par byed-pa chenmo or *Mahavyutpati*. To study the translation works prior to the standardization of the Tibetan language, the study of old and new terms of orthography, written by Pen-chen Sakya Chog, Mindrug Lo-tsa-va, Pekhang Lo-tsa-va is very essential.

A few examples of the old and new terms are given here for the clear understanding :

spa-lo	*spob-pa*
smre	*sdug-bsnal*
nan-tur	*nan-tan*
gyar-len	*khas-len*
mu-cor	*rdzun*
ne-sho-med-pa	*skyon-med-pa*
rkam-pa	*shen-chags-che-ba*
phya-le-ba	*khyod-mnam-pa*

The hChe-med mZod [Amarakoṣa] is an important work for the studies of Tibetan equivalent of Snaskrit. Some examples given here which will help us to know the differences easily:

chaitra = dpyid-' brid
basanta = dpyid-ka
vaishakha = sa-zla
shuklapaksa = dkar-phyogs

In the third stage, the beginning of 13th century, flourished the great hierarchy of Sakya who obtained the influence over Tibet. Among the most known scholars of the time were Sakya Pandita Kungah Gyaltsan, Dogon Phag-pa, Shong-ston Lo-tsa-va; and they have introduced the five sciences of knowledge-Rig-Ngas Inga after thoroughly studying the Kalapa Vyakarana, Chandra Vyakarana, Kab-bya and so on from the great Indian scholars. This is known as Rig ngai chung-va nga, that is five minor science of literature. In order to study not only Tibetan language and literature but also sutdies of gso-va rigpa [medicine], nang-don rigpa [Buddhist Philosophy], bzo rigpa [technical subjects] etc. one must study these five minor sciences.

Here I would like to quote some of the most common verses written by great scholars:

(A) From Chu-Shing sTan-bchos by dkon-mchog bstan-pai sgronme:

chu-phran-brgal-bar-mi-nus-des
rgya-mtsho-rkyal-gyis-ga-la-chod /
ya-rabs-lugs-kyan-mi-shes-na
chos-kyi-de-nid-di-ltar-rtogs //

This verse is written simile on water; and it is the very common verse of six syllables;

(B) It is from *Sa-Kya legs-gshad* by Sa-kya Pandita:

mkhas-pa-brtsad-cid-ma-dris-par
de-yi-bar-du-gtin-mi-dpog
rna-la-dbu-gus-ma-bsnun-bar
de-srid-gshan-dan-kyad-dri-yod //

Here the depth of the knowledge of a well-versed man is compared with that of a drum; and is written in one of the common verse of seven syllables.

(C) Verse from dbyangs-chen dgyas-glu; it is an example of the 17th Simile, bsngags-pai-dpe:

mi-bsrun-glags-lta'i-rgol-dan-rab-'jomas-shid
blo-gsal-tshogs-rnams-chos-kyis-tshim-byed-pa'i
thogs-med-sku-mched-ji-bshin-dzod-kha-pa
ltar-bdras-skye-dgu' i-gdrug-na-mdon-par-mdzes //

(D) From the verse of Bo'i-Khaspa; it is written on metaphr: 13th rGyue-gzugs-chen:

khyod-ni-phan-pas-snoms-phyin-ni-ma-dan
bdud-kyi-las-kun-'dzoms-pas-dpa'-bo-ste
'gro-rnams-'khor-bar-mi-ltur-'chel-ba'i-rten
yid-la-re-ba-ster-bas-nor-bu'n-lags //

(E) Lyrical sound: by Dharshab, it is written in 8 syllables:

gnas-ri-rva-bas-bskor-ba'i-shin-khams
gnas-ljonas-bod-ni-'dzam-glin-yonas-la
ran-ran-skad-dan-chas-gos-gan-nas
ran-btsan-gtsan-ma'i-rna-bo-grags-so //

In short : the Poems are written in the pattern of:

12/34/56; 12/34/56-7; 1-23/45/67-8; 12/34/56/78; 123/45/6 78/9 10; 12/34/56-7/8 9 10; 1-2345/67-8/9 10; 12/34/56/789/10 11; 12/34-5/67/89/10 11; and so on.

Thus Poems of highly classical or literary are in 11 to 15; sometimes even 27.

Though the gramatical function of Tibetan is closely related to Sanskrit, Tibetan should tauhght by our own method, and not as Sanskrit, or English which over simplifies. Above all these days many new books and journals written in modern Tibetan, are keeping the standard of the language. Hence, it is so important to study the language pattern of both classical and modern Tibetan.

In short many of the Sanskrit texts have been lost and destroyed in India, and the original texts are found in Tibetan. Hence, the Tibetan literature is the main source of Buddhist studies. And, to understand the great treasure of Buddhism—both *Tantra* and *Sutra*; the five minor sciences-Rig-gnas Chung-va-Nga should be studied thoroughly.

Professor Tucci's Work in the Field of Buddhist Logic

14

Heramba Chatterjee Shastri

Rabindranath Tagore realised the necessity of forming a brotherhood of Indologists of the oriental and occidental specialists specially when the concept of Visva-Bharati loomed large in his mind. During his foreign tours he accordingly availed himself of the opportunities of meeting them and inviting them to accept visiting Professorships at his contemplated University. He met Levy at Paris in 1920 and requested him to be the first Visiting Professor and during his stay Prof. Levy initiated the study of Chinese and Tibetan here. Visva-Bharati was inaugurated in 1921 (Bengali year, 1328) and the next prominent European Indologist, M. Winternitz was persuaded to accept Visiting Professorship here in 1922. He enriched the study of Sanskrit literature by his History of Indian Literature in three volumes, besides several research papers in different fields of Indology. Prof. Tucci had his share of contribution to unearth specially the wonderful treasures of Buddhist Literature which were inaccessible to the oriental scholars of India, since they were preserved in Tibetan and Chinese translations, the two languages which were not cultured in India except in Santiniketan, where the impetus came from the association of these European Indologists.

Paying obeisance to these three pioneers (*purvebhyah pathikrdbhyah.* R.V. X. 14. 15) it is being humbly submitted:

munitrayam idam natva tadgranthan paribhavya ca /
nyayabaudda-siddhanta-nibandho 'yam viracyate //

Logical texts, specially the Buddhist logical texts are like veritable ocean with saline water, unapproachable owing to tumults and uproars of the commentators. Should not then the water be drunk? Certainly intelligent person like cloud deserve to drink the same :

nyayambudhi-r-didhitikara-yukti-kallola-kolahala-durvigahah /
tasyapi patum na payah samarthah, kim nama dhimat-pratibhambuvahah //

Dinnaga is rightly regarded as the father of mediaeval logic. He was regarded as the strongest opponent of the Brahmanical logicians and rather abusive words and expressions were hurled against him. Udyotakara in the introductory verse of his *Nyayavarttika* observes :

yad aksapadah pravaro muninam
samaya sastram jagato jagada /
kutarkika jnana-nivrttihetuh
karisyate tasya maya nibandhah //

Texts like his *Pramana-Samuccaya* were composed in Sanskrit, the original of which is lost, but fortunately for us, it is preserved in Tibetan translation. (The first chapter has been restored into Sanskrit and edited by H.R.R. Iyengar, Mysore University Publication, Mysore, 1930).

It is distributed over six chapters : perception, inference for one's own self (*svarthanumana),* inference for others *(pararthanumana*), reason and example (*hetudrstanta),* negation of the opposite (*apoha)* and analogue *(jati*). His definition of perception as also other cases like *apoha* were characterised by distinctiveness and the Hindu logicians took great pains to refute the points of Dinnaga. Thus he defines perception that which, being freed from preconception, is unconnected with name, genus etc. :

pratyaksam kalpanapodham namajatyasamyutam.

This has been quoted by the Hindu logician Udyotakara who has vehemently criticised the whole theory of Perception by Dinnaga.

His other text is *Nyayapravesa,* which also is preserved in Tibetan (This was edited in the G.O. Series, but very informative article on the authorship of the text was contributed in the *Journal of Royal Asiatic Society* by Tucci under the title: *"Is Nyayapravesa by Dignaga"*, in 1928). Another small treatise on logic is *Hetucakra-hamaru* by Dinnaga, whose Sanskrit original is lost, but a Tibetan translation is preserved. Similarly the *Pramana-samuccayavrtti,* an auto-commentary by Dinnaga on his own text is preserved in Tibetan.

The *Nyayamukha* by Dinnaga has been edited by Tucci in 1930 under the title. : The *Nyayamukha* of Dignnaga, being the oldest Buddhist text on logic after Chinese and Tibetan materials. This has been published from Heidelberg. In the same year (i.e. 1930) Tucci delivered the Readership Lecture in the Calcutta University, which was published in the form of a book : *On some aspects of the doctrines of Maitreyanatha and Asanga.* In the *Journal of the Royal Asiatic Society,* he published in the same year : A fragment from the *Pratityasamutpada-vyakhya* of Vasubandhu. In 1929 the fruits of the efforts, specially because of his exceptional knowledge of Chinese and Tibetan, found expression in his publication, in the *Pre-Dinnaga Buddhist texts on Logic from Chinese sources,* in the preface of which he has addressed his friend Vidhusekhara Sastri, explaining his reasons for translating into Sanskrit the text, namely, *Upayahrdaya* generally attributed to Nagarjuna. It was translated into Chinese twice.

The text is interesting since in it interesting points relating to *vada* have been raised. Thus, in replay to the point raised : *tasmat svahita-parahitabhitabhilasenaite vivadadharmah praheyah,* replay has been given thus: *yadiha loke vado na bhaved, mugdhanam bahulyam syat. Tatas ca laukika-mithya-jnana–kusalata-sahacara-bhranti-samudbhuta-kukarma-bhih samsaradurgatih sadarthahanis ca.* p.1.

It has been contended further : *yathamraphala-paripustikamena tat-phala-pariraksanartham bahir. bahutara-tiksna-kantaka-nikara-vinyasah kriyate. vadarambho' pi tathaivadhuna saddharma-raksanecchaya na tu khyatilabhaya...................... dharmaraksanartham eva hi vada arabdhavyah.*

It is in this text we may get suggestion that four types of *pramanas* could be restored to establish a point : *arthasthapanam icchata caturvidhan jnanam asrayitavyam. kim tac caturvidham ? pratyaksam anumanam upamanam agamas ca.* p. 6.

He has retranslated into Sanskrit another text entitled *Tarkasastra* (Nanjio 1252 : See Bagchi, *Le canon Buddhique on Chine,* 1.p 423 (6)) attributed to Vasubandhu. The work was translated into Chinese by Paramartha and a commentary on the same, which is lost. The text is very difficult and the mode of treatment is also characterised by novelty. The notes added to the Sanskrit rendering make the translation scholastic and valuable.

He has also translated into English with exhaustive notes and references from the Chinese and Tibetan sources the *Vigrahavyavartani* and the text is of great importance since in it we find how Nagarjuna explains the fundamental tenets of his *Sunyavada* refuting the objections raised against him by his opponents.

Tucci has translated into English from the Chinese sources the *Satasastra* by Aryadeva and the text is important in the sense that we find here interesting discussions on the concept of *Sunyata*. By making reference to the doctrines of the Samkhya School as propagated by Kapila, as also to the texts of the Vaisesikas, it has been held that in short the doctrine of Buddha may be described as of two varieties, that stopping evils *(papa)* and of practising the good acts *(kusala-karma)*.

Tucci edited along with Pt. Vidhusekhar Bhattacarya the *Madhyanta-vibhaga sutra-bhasya-tika* of Sthiramati in the Calcutta Oriental Series. No. XXIV, in 1932.

In the same year he published in the G.O.S. (No. 62): The commentaries on the *Prajnaparamita* : The *Abhisamayalamkaraloka* of Haribhadra. In 1934, he contributed very informative paper on the *Ratnavali of Nagarjuna* in the *Journal of the Royal Asiatic Society*, London. In 1947, in the same Journal (*J.R.A.S*) he wrote on : *The Prajnaparamita-pindartha of Dignaga.*

In earlier years, we may refer to his Italian translation of Rajasekhara's *Karpuramanjari* (in 1922) and his informative notes on the *Divyavadana*. In 1923 his works were published on these three topics of importance : (a) *Saptasati-prajnaparamita*, (b) *Lankavatara*-studies, (c) *Biography of Nagarjuna*

He contributed very scholastic notes on the *Saundarananda-kavya* of Asvaghosa in 1925.

An explorer and traveller Prof. Tucci undertook eight expeditions to Tibet from 1929 and in between 1950 and 1954 as many as six expeditions were conducted by him to Nepal, and the results of his academic pursuits have found expressions in the Seven Volumes of Indo-Tibetica (1932-1941) and three volumes of *Tibetan Painted Scrolls* (1949).

Tribute to the memories of this polyglot Indologist cannot be complete unless reference is made to the highly scholastic Journal *East and West,* which has been enriched profusedly by his writings and which has earned world-wide celebrity by the rich contributions from eminent scholars.

Finally, reference should also be made to the series of texts under the heading : *Minor Buddhist Texts,* Parts, I and II (Published on the occasion of the Buddha Jayanti, from Kyoto, in 1978)

1. Text : *Prajñāpāramita* by Aryasanga : out of 300 stanzas 77 have been translated into English alongwith Tibetan texts.
2. Analysis of the *Vajracchedikā* according to Vasubandhu (Taisho 1510) (compared with Kamalasila's commentary)
3. *Aryāṣṭa-sāhasrikāyāh prajñāpāramitāyāh piṇḍārthah* (Sanskrit texts, Tibetan translation and English translation)
4. *Catuhstava-samāsārtha* of Amrtakara
5. *Hetu-tattvopadeśa* of Jitari and *Tarkasopāna* of Vidyakarasanti.
6. The Sanskrit and Tibetan texts of the First *Bhāvanākrama.*

Hetutattvopadesa: A Study

15

Narendra Kumar Dash

During the reign of the king Sron-tsen gam-po, Buddhism established in Tibet for the first time. He married the princesses of Nepal and China, who were strong followers of Buddhism. But the actual spread of *Dharma* began only after the arrival of three Indian scholars viz., Santaraksita, Padmasambhava and Kamalasila.[1] During this time a large number of works on Buddhist Religion, as well as other subjects like Grammar, Logic, Poetics and literary works etc. were translated into Tibetan from Indian literature by many great scholars, from both India and Tibet. However, the translation from Indian Literature on a large scale did not commence before the second half of eighth century A.D. These translation activities particularly furthered after the establishment of the first Tibetan monastery i.e. Bsam-yas (circa 775), combined with the acceptance of Buddhism as a state religion.

It would seem that the patronage for translation activities stimulated its centralization and standardization. A Central Committee of translators comprising of both Indian and Tibetan Scholars, was constituted. They were authorised to revise old and new translations in order to attain uniformity in terminology, and translation techniques. This committee is generally referred to as *Bcom-ldan-'das-kyi-rin-lugs-kyi-'dun-sa.*[2] It is known from the historical records that compositions of the scholars such as Panini, Candragomin, Dinnaga, Nagarjuna, Asanga, Maitreya, Vasubandhu, Dharmakirtti and Dharmottara, etc. were included in Tibetan translation. Some valuable Indian works on different subjects, which are not found now in their original form, are also preserved in the Tibetan translations. Thus, the works of Acarya Jitari are also found in the Tibetan translation and here, for our practical purpose we will discuss only one text of Jitari, entitled the *Hetutattvopadesa,* which is a fundamental work on Buddhist logic.

Jitari, the author of the *Hetutattvopadesa,* was a very prolific writer and was considered as one of the greatest Pandits of the Mediaeval Bengal. The works which are credited to the name Jitari were composed in different subjects viz., *Nyaya, Tantra* and *Sadhana* etc.[3] In the Taranatha's *History of Buddhism in India*, Chattopadhyaya, has given a list of twenty-three works in her supplementary note no. 72, which are credited to the name Jitari. Beside, Prof. Tucci has edited a *nyaya* work of Jitari and the work was published in the Annals of Bhandarkar Oriental Research Institute, vol. XI in 1930. The name of the work is : *Jatinirakriti*. Thus a total number of twenty-four works were composed by Jitari (note–1).

The spelling of the name of the author of the *Hetutattvopadesa* in modern works is usually Jetari. In the colophon of the *Hetutattvopadesa* the name is Jetari viz, *mkhas-pa-chen-po-dse-ta-ri 'i shal-sna-nas mdsad-pa-rdsogs-go//.*[4] In some other works the spelling is Jetari. In the modern works also we find this name. Vidyabhusana,[5] Dey,[6] and Roerich[7] prefer to spell the name Jetari. Though Sankrtyayana prefers the name as Jetari, still in one of his articles he uses the word Jitari.[8] It appears that the spelling of Jetari is based upon the Tibetan texts which contain some information about the author and on the colophons of the *Bstan- 'gyur* as well.

On the other hand, in the colophons of the two Sanskrit works of our author, which have been edited by Prof. Tucci, we find the name Jitari viz., *Jatinirakrtiriyam jitaripadanam* and *hetutattvopadesah samaptah/[9] krtir iyam panditaraja-jitaripadanam //.* [10] The Tibetan equivalent of the Sanskrit word Jitari is : *dgra-las rnam-rgyal* and the Sanskrit word seems to be the perfect form. Our remark is also supported by the fact that the name Jitari is also a title of the Buddha himself. In this connection it may not be out of context to quote a verse from the *Trikandasesa* of Purusottama Deva, where Jitari has been mentioned as a name of Buddha viz.,

buddho 'kanisthaga-mahamuni-dhrmacakra
ragasaris-trisaranah khasamo dasarhah /
tapi gunakaramahasukha-vajrinas-ca
maitribalasama-jitari-samanta bhadrah// [11]

In the commentary called Sarartha Candrika, it has been said that *jitah parajitah arayah ragadiklesah yena sah (jitari).*[12] This explanation of Mahathera is quite similar to the Tibetan spelling mentioned above. Thus, it may be concluded that the correct spelling of the name is Jitari and not Jetari or Jetari.

Now a natural question arises as to whether all the twenty-four works of different subjects were composed by single and identical author or written by different authors of the same name. Earlier, this problem also attracted the notice of Prof. Tucci and Dey. Though in the introduction to the edition of the *Jatinirakriti* Tucci is silent about the said problem, still in his introduction to the *Hetutattvopadesa*, he discusses the mentioned problem in detail. After a long discussion, he concludes that there were two authors with the same name of Jitari : a Jitari and a Mahajitari and the younger one was chiefly a Tantric author. Prior to Tucci, Dey also suggested about two Jitaris. He says that "with regard to Jetari, the next important writer, the Tibetan tradition appears to distinguish a senior and a junior sage of that name. The senior or Mahajetari belonged to Varendra, where his father Garbhapada lived at the court of king Sanatana. He is said to have received from Mahapala the Diploma of the Pandita of Vikramasila Vihara, and instructed Dipamkara Srijnana in the Buddhist lore. The younger Jetari was a Buddhist Tantric sage of Bengal, who initiated Bodhibhagya and gave him the name *Lavanyavajra.* It is possible that the three learned works on Buddhist Logic, preserved in Tibetan, belonged to the Senior Jetari"[13]. This remark of Dey needs some study. Dey opines that the younger Jetari was a Buddhist Tantric sage of Bengal and he initiated Bodhibhagya and gave him the name *Lavanyavajra.* But in the Sum-pa mkhan-po's history we have a story where he narrates that Jitari was said to have been a disciple of *dpal sde* (Skt. Srisena) and the master of *Byan-chub skal-ldan* (skt. Bodhibhagya) and he gave the name *sGeg-pa'i rdo-rje (Skt. Lalita-Vajra / Lilavajra).* We prefer to reconstruct the Tibetan word as *Lilavajra.* Accroding to S.C.Das *sGeg-pa'i-rdo-rje* (*Lavanyavajra, Lilavajra*) is the name of a Buddhist sage of Ancient India who visited Udyana (Ancient Cabul) and spread Buddhism there.[14] However, in the history of Buddhism in India we are not familiar with the name *Lavanyavajra,* but with *Lalita-vajra* and *Lilavajra* who are quite familiar in Tantric Buddhism. Taranath's history suggests that Lalitavajra was a siddhayogi during the period of Sri Dharmkirti and he was a great Pandita of Nalendra. His disciple *Lilavajra* committed to writing the works of his master. But the *Yamantakodaya* and the *Santikrodhavikridita* etc. were composed by *Lilavajra,* the great. Therefore, the name given by Jitari may not *Lavanyavajra,* but may be either *Lalitavajra* or *Lilavajra.* However, Prof. Tucci prefers to reconstruct the name as *Lilavajra.* Again, Dey opines that the three learned works on Logic belonged to the Senior Jitari. But we have four works on Buddhist Logic which are credited to Jitari. We presume that the work *Jatinirakriti*, edited by Prof. Tucci, was not known to Dey and his remark in this context is based on the Tibetan translations only.

Accroding to Taranatha the Pandita *Lalitavajra* was contemporary of Dharmakirtti. As Dharmakirtti was a disciple of Dhrmapala, who was a Professor in Nalanda at the time when the Chinese pilgrim Hiuen Tsang visited it. Lalitavajra's time may be placed in the lst quarter of the Seventh Century A.D. Again, the time of *Lilavajra*, the disciple of Lalitavajra, may be around the first half of the Eighth Century A.D. Since Jitari was the master of either of these two he might have flourished about 8th century A.D. This is also supported by Sum-pa mkhan-po. He says that Jitari was the teacher of *Byan-chub skal-ldan*, who was given the name *Sges-pa'i-rdo-rje*, was a contemporary of Ra-sa-pa-la.[15] Vidyabhusana suggests Rasapala's time as : 753 A.D. to 765 A.D. on the basis of Taranath's history.[16]

Again, it has been mentioned that Jitari was the teacher of Atisa Dipamkara. According to Rahula Sankrtyayana, Dipamkara created special problems for his early education. When the young prince Candragarbha first met Jitari and the latter asked him who he was, Candragarbha replied that he was the son of the master of the land. Jitari thought that this answer showed pride. We neither have any master nor any slave. If you are the ruler of the land, then go away, he answered. Very humbly Candragarbha told him that he wanted to renounce the world. At this, Jitari advised him to go to Nalanda, as he thought that if the prince was ordained too close to his father's capital, it would be difficult for him to overcome pride.[17]

It has been accepted that Atisa was born in the 'water-male-horse' year i.e. the 1039 Vikrama era, i.e. 982 A.D.[18] and since Jitari, who was living in a cottage close to the capital of the father of Dipamkara, was the teacher of

Candragarbha, we may say that he was flourished in the later half of the 10th century. In this context Sankrtyayana suggests : "Jitari was renowned as a grammarian and erudite scholar".[19] However, still now we have no information, neither from Tibetan source or from Indian source, to suggest that Jitari was a grammarian. Not a single work on grammar, which is credited to Jitari, is available now. But it is known from the history of Taranath that Jitari, learnt, without studying the scripts, all the fine arts, prosody, *Sabdavidya* (grammar) etc.

Thus on the basis of our study, we may suggest that there were two authors in the mediaeval periods with an identical name i.e. Jitari. The Senior one was flourished about 8th century A.D. and the junior Jitari was flourished in 10th century A.D. Again, the elder one was the disciple of *dpal-sde* and the master of *Lalitavajra* or *Lilavajra*. The young one was the master of Atisa Dipamkara, when he was a boy. But we have no information as to which one was the Buddhist Logician. If we agree with the view of Dey, then the Senior Jitari was the great logician. Vidyabhusana, however, does not mention about two Jitaris.[20] According to his observation, Jitari received the royal Diploma of Pandita of the University of Vikramasila from the king Mahapala. "Maha-pala reigned upto 940 A.D. and Dipamkara was born in 980 A.D. Their contemporary, Jetari (Jitari), must have lived between these dates".

Works

It has been said earlier that twenty-four works are credited to the name of Jitari and again, it is also mentioned that the Buddhist Logician Jitari, the Senior, had composed four works on Logic. Thus, it is natural that the rest twenty works were composed by the Junior Jitari, the teacher of Candragarbha. Vidyabhusana,[21] like Dey, mentions that the author had composed three works. It seems that Vidyabhusana was not aware of the work *Jatinirakrti* which was edited in 1930.

The Hetutattvopadesa

The text *Hetutattvopadesa* was edited for the first time by Durgacharan Chattopadhyaya with a Sanskrit reconstruction on the basis of the xylographs of the Narthang and Peking versions and was published by Calcutta University in 1939. Again a Sanskrit version of the same text has been edited in the roman scripts by Prof. Tucci in his work entitled *Minor Buddhist Texts*, published from Roma in 1956. Accroding to Prof. Tucci, his edition is based upon a palmleaf manuscript, which was presented to him by the abbot of the monastery Khongdkandzong *(dGon dkar rdson),* which is situated in the southern bank of the Tsangpo river. Before Tucci, the Sanskrit version of this work was not known to the academic world and therefore, Vidyabhusana remarks that the Sanskrit original of this work appears to be lost.

Translators

It is known from the colophon of the work under discussion that it was translated into Tibetan by the Indian Pandita Kumarakalasa in collaboration with a Tibetan interpreter, Bhiksu Sakyaprabha, viz., *rgyagar-gyi-mkhan-po Pandi-ta ku-ma-ra-ka-la-sa-dan / lo-tsa-ba dge-slon Sakya-od-kyis-bsgyur-cin shus-nas-gtan-la-phab-pa'o //.* It may reconstructed into Sanskrit as : *bharatiya upadhayena panditene kumarakalasene bhasantarakarena bhiksuna sakyaprabhena (bhotbhasayam) samsodhyam ca vinyasthah.//*

Date of Translation

It is not known either from the colophon or from the text

that when and where the said work was translated and revised. However we have some information about Kumarakalasa, the translator. The Blue Annals shows that Kumarakalasa was also the translator of the work *Phags-pa 'jam-dpal-gyi-rtsa-ba'i rgyud* (Skt. *Arya-manjusri-mula tantra)*. The Tibetan Lo-tsa-ba of the translation of the said work was Bhiksu Sakya blo-gras (Skt. Sakyabodhi)[22]. Roerich, again suggests that the said Tantra was translated into Tibetan by order of Iho-btsun-pa Gbyan-chub' od (Skt. Bodhiprabha) at the monastery of *Tho-lin* in Guge[23]. The king Bodhiprabha was the royal disciple of Atisa. Thus Kumarakalasa was flourished in the 11th century, as the king Bodhiprabha was a contemporary to Nayapala of Bengal (1030-55 A.D.).[24]

Again, Bu-ston, the famous historian, after describing the activities of Atisa in Tibet (1042-1054 A.D.), mentions a long list of the Indian Pandits, those translated a great number of texts into Tibetan along with the help of the different Lo-tsa-bas.[25] It is also known from the same source that Kumarakalasa taught at *San-dun-ne'u-thog* and other places.[26]

The co-translator of the work under discussion is Bhiksu Sakyaprabha. Bu-ston says that the translators who had first been with the great Master and, moreover, Sakyaprabha, *Yol-cog Dorje-van-chug, Ge-va'e-lo-do* translated a great number of works.[27] Thus, both Kumarakalasa and Sakyaprabha were contemporary to Atisa Dipamkara and, therefore the translation of the work *Hetutattvopadesa* was made in the 11th century A.D. However, due to the want of evidences, we are not sure that where the translation was made.

Vidyabhusana, in his work : *History of Indian Logic'*, suggests that the title *Hetutattvopadesa* signifies "instruction on the real nature of the middle term in a syllogism". This seems to be an oversight, as the present work sets out to discuss the problems which cover almost the entire scope of any work on Logic. The word *hetu* has been used here in a wider sense of reasoning on logic in general and not in the sense of the mark *(linga)* or in 'the middle term' of a syllogistic reasoning.

This small work of Jitari opens with the introductory verse :

sadhanam dusanam caiva sabhasam parasamvide /
pratyaksam anumaṇam ca sabhasam tvatmasamvide //

This introductory verse hints that the problem have classified in this work into *sadhana* "demonstration", *dusana* "refutation", *pratyaksa* "perception" and *anumana* "inference". Thus at the beginning of the work the author says that demonstration and refutation together with their fallacies are useful in arguing with others *(parasamvide);* Perception and Inference together with their fallacies are useful for one's own illumination *(atmasamvide).* It is interesting to note that this opening verse of Jitari also occurs in the beginning of the *Nyayapravesa* of Acarya Dinnaga.[29] In this work of Dinnaga, the term *sadhana* has been defined as the presentation of *paksa, hetu,* and *drstanta* and therefore it has been said in the text that : *paksadivacanani sadhanam.*[30] *Sadhana* undoubtedly involves *anumana,* but this is evidently *pararthanumana,* being intended for the convication of other than one's own self. It is, therefore, different from *anumana* in the second line of the verse, which is but *svarthanumana* and bring convication to one's own self. When there is any error in any of the three members i.e. *paksa, hetu* and *drstanta* of a syllogism, it will be a case of *sadhanabhasa, dusana* consists in pointing out some defect in the adversary's arguments. *Dusanabhasa* is a false refutation and is equivalent to *jati* viz., *dusanabhaso dusanameveti sa prativadinocyate / yada purvapaksavadino 'bhutam dosamudbhavayati (tada) sa dusanabhaso jatiriti.*[31]

In the *Pramana samuccaya* (PS) Dinnaga argues in support of two *pramanas,* i.e. *pratyaksa* and *anumana.* Here the author of the PS, perhaps attacks Aksapada, who propounded four *pramanas*. Accroding to Dinnaga the objects of knowledge *(prameya)* are of two kinds i.e. *svalaksana* 'the unique self-characteristic' and *samanyalaksana* 'the generic class-characteristic'[32] and with reference to these two kinds of *prameyas* two *pramanas, pratyaksa* and *anumana* are requisitioned.[33] We apprehened the *svalaksana* aspect of things by the former, which is perceptible and by the later the *samanyalaksana* which is imperceptible *(paroksa)*. Therefore, the author of the *Sarvadarsana-samgraha* rightly says that :

na pratyaksaparoksabhyam meyasyanyasya sambhavah/
tasmat prameyadvitvenapramanadvitvam isyate //.[34]

Dinnaga does not give any formal definition of Perception, which is well known as the knowledge of objects derived through the channel of the senses. But he describes Perception as that which, being freed from preconception is unconnected with name genus etc.[35] For the example suppose a person in twilight mistakes a rope for a snake, his knowledge of the snake is a preconception and is not an act of Perception. Dinnaga contends that Perception is not connected with the name, as we can perceive a thing without knowing its name. It is also not connected with genus, so that the Perception of a thing consists of the knowledge of its individual characteristics along. "Suppose I see a cow. This cow, which I see, is a peculiar one. Its infinite peculiarities can only be realised by one who have seen it. If proceed to indicate this cow to other persons by saying that I saw a cow which is named *Dittha* or which is red, etc., I can only convey to those persons the idea of a cow of a certain class, that is, a cow possessing the common characteristics of a class of cows, but can never express to them the individual cow which I saw. Hence it follows that Perception cannot be properly expressed by name, genus etc."[36]

In the *Nyayabindu* of Dharmakirtti, the word *Samyakjnanam* 'valid knowledge' has been used for *pramana*, as all objects of man are accomplished by perfect or valid knowledge. This is of two kinds :-Perception and Inference.[37] Again Perception is that, where the knowledge derived through the senses, etc. and devoid of error (*abhranta*).[38] Pre-conception refers to the experiences of false images which appear real as if they were capable of being addressed and touched, e.g. the shadow of a tree may appear as the tree itself or a rope may appear as snake. Error is caused by such causes as darkness, quick motion, journey by boat, shaking etc.; for instance, to a man journeying boat, trees on both banks appear to move.

Jitari, however, without naming any one of these two famous Buddhist Logicians, accepts the first word of Dinnaga i.e. *Kalpana* and adds the word *abhranta* of Dharmakirtti to it. Thus, he says that : *pratyaksam kalpanapodham-abhrantam* and therefore, he is supporting the arguments given by Dharmakirtti.

Dinnaga's idea of *kalpana* in the sense of *jatyadiyojana* has been rejected by his successors on the ground that *jati* or *samanya,* being itself unreal and untenable according to Buddhist Philosophy, need not be precluded by any special mention, as this would imply its reality.

While Dharmakirtti argues in favour of four kinds of Perception,[39] Jitari says that there are three kinds viz., *tatra pratyaksam trividham.* They are (i) Perception by the five senses (*vyavaharikamindriyajnanam);* (ii) self-consciousness (*sarvacittacaittanamatmasamvedanam*) *and* (iii) knowledge of a contemplative saint *(bhutarbhavanasphutaprakar-saparyantajam yogijnanam).* Here, Jitari not only accepts the divisions of Perception (without the second one i.e. Perception by the mind) made by Dharamkirtti, but writes down the lines from his *Nyayabindu*. He omits *manovijnana* probably on the ground that it has a mere scriptural rather than a logical justification. Dharmottara remarks *monovijnana* is approved by scriptural authority devoid of all argumentative support, but nevertheless it can be justified when explained after Dharmakirtti: *etacca siddhanta prasiddham manasa-pratyaksam natvasya prasadhakam asti pramanam evamjatiyakam tad yadi syan na kascid dosah syat iti vaktum laksanamakhyatam asyeti.*[40]

It has been indicated in the introductory verse of the *Hetutattvopadesa* that the Inference is of two kinds : *svarthanumana* and *pararthanumana.* These divisions of Inference are also, earlier, mentioned by Dinnaga. According to him, inference for one's self (*svarthanumana)* is defined as the knowledge of a thing derived through its mark on sign of three characters [41] viz., *karya* 'effect' *(Tib 'bras-bu); svabhava* 'identity' (*Tib. Ran-bshin*); and *anupalabdhi,* 'non-perception' *(Tib. mi-dmigs-pa).* Thus, the mark may be an effect of the thing to be inferred; e.g. smoke of fire; the mark may be in essence identical with the thing to be inferred; e.g. a *simsapa* identical with a tree and non-perception of the mark be due to the non-perception of a pot is a mark of non-existence thereof. Jitari also accepts the same logic as given by Dinnaga.

The *pararthanumana* or 'the Inference for the sake others' takes place when a person demonstrates to others the conclusion drawn by him through as Inference of one's self and therefore, Jitari says : *trirupahetupradarsena paravagamanimittam krta prayogah pararthanumana-mityucyate*[42]. Again, this is of two kinds : (a) positive *(sadharmya*) and (b) negative *(vaidharmya*). Jitari explains these two with fine examples. In the case of first, he argues, sound is non-eternal, because it is a product, all products are non-eternal as a pot (positive)[43]. In the case of the latter, sound is non-eternal i.e. eternal is a product, no non-non eternal i.e. eternal is a product as ether (negative)[44].

After explaining the *sadhya* and *sadhana*, Jitari explains the middle term *(hetu)*. According to his arguments the three forms of the *hetu* are the following :—

1. The middle term must abide in the minor term (*paksa sattvam*) e.g. the sound is non-eternal, because it is a product, like a pot, but unlike ether.
2. This middle term must abide only in cases which are homologous with the major term, e.g. in the above reasoning *'krtakatva'* abides in a pot which is homologous with things which have no eternity.
3. And the middle term must never abide in cases which are heterologous from the major term, e.g. in the above reasoning *'krtakatva'*.does not abide in ether which is heterologous from things that have no-eternity.

Thus Jitari explains about the fallacies of the middle term *(hetvabhasa)*[45]. They are *asiddha* 'un-proved', *viruddha* 'contradictory' and *anaikantika* 'un-certain' viz., *hetvabhasastrividhah / asiddho viruddho'naikantikasca*[46] *//.* That, where the *paksa* is un-proved, is *asiddha-hetvabhasa.*[47] In the reasoning sound is eternal, because it is visible. Similarly in the reasoning the hill has fire, because it has vapour; vapour as an effect of the fire is questioned. Where the cause *(hetu)* is contradictory to the *sadhya,* that is *viruddha-hetvabhasa.*[48] In the reasoning sound is eternal, because it is a product', 'product' is not homogeneous with 'eternal' and that is in the middle term is opposed to the major term. Lastly, the *hetu* where *sapaksa, vipaksa* are present or not present or where there is doubt about these two, is called *anaikantikahetvabhasa.*[49] In the reasoning 'sound is non-eternal, because it is knowledge', the knowledge is too general, because it includes the eternal as well as the non-eternal.

From the above discussion, it is proved that the work composed by Jitari is not a work dedicated to the middle term only, but it covers almost all aspects of logic.

References and Notes

1. Refer Shakabpa, T.W.D., *Tibet: A Political History*, Yale University Press, 1967.
2. Refer Dash, N.K., *A Survey on Sanskrit Grammar in Tibetan Language,* Delhi, 1993, p. 3.
3. Refer the supplementary note no.72 of the English translation of the history of Buddhism in India, written by Taranatha; the said work has been translated by Lama Chimpa and Alaka Chattopadhyaya and edited by Debiprasad Chattopadhyaya; for the works of Jitari. However, one more i.e. *Jatinirakrti* of Jitari, has not been included in the list. Also see note-1.
4. Refer the colophon of the *Hetutattvopadesa*, edited by Chattopadhyay, D., Calcutta; 1939, p. 63.
5. Vidyabhusana, S.C., *History of Indian Logic;* p. 337.
6. Dey, S.K., Sanskrit Literature in the book *History of Bengal*, Volume One, Hindu Period, ed. R. C. Majumdar, reprint 1971, p. 334.

   Prof. Tucci thinks that R. C. Majumdar writes as Jitari. Actually this is the option of S. K. Dey as he is the writer of the portion where the author Jitari is referred. But that has been edited by Majumdar.
7. Roerich, G.N., *The Blue Annals*, Part I and II bound together, Reprint-Delhi, 1988, p. 243.
8. Refer, Sankrtyayana, R, Acarya Dipamkara Srijnana in *2500 Years of Buddhism,* ed. by Bapat, P.V., New Delhi, 1956. p. 200.
9. Tucci, G, (ed.) *Jatinirakrti* in the *Annals of Bhandarkar Oriental Research Institute (ABORI),* Vol. XI, 1930. p. 58.
10. Tucci, G, (ed). Hetutattvopadesa in the *Minor Buddhist Texts*, pt.1, Roma, 1956, p. 274.

11. Mahathera, C. A. S, (ed) *The Trikandasesa of Purusottamadeva*, Bombay, 1919, p. 4
12. *Ibid.*, p. 4.
13. Refer, *History of Bengal*, ed. R.C. Majumdar, p. 334.
14. Refer, Das, S.C, *Tibetan-English Dictionary*, (compact edition), Delhi, 1985, p.322.
15. Vide, Tucci, G, *Minor Buddhist Texts*, Pt.One, 1956, p.250.
16. Refer, Vidyabhusana, S.C., *History of Indian Logic*, 1971, p.577.
17. Vide, Chattopadhyaya, A., *Atisa and Tibet*, Calcutta, 1967, pp. 65-66.
18. *Ibid.*, p. 66.
19. Sankrtyayana, R, *Acarya Dipamkara Srijnana*, 1956, p. 200.
20. Vidyabhusana, S.C., *History of Indian Logic*, 1971, 337.
21. *Ibid.*, p. 337.
22. Roerich, G. N, *The Blue Annals*, p. X.
23. *Ibid.*, p. X.
24. Chattopadhyay, A., *Atisa and Tibet*, p. 54.
25. Obermiller, E., *History of Buddhism by Bu-ston*, pt.II (English translation), Heidelberg, 1932, pp. 215-216.
26. *Ibid.*, p. 216.
27. *Ibid.*, p. 214.
28. Vidyabhusana, S.C., *History of Indian Logic*, 1971, 337
29. Cf, *sadhanam dusanam caiva sabhasam paarsamvide /*

    pratyayaksamanumanam ca sabhasam tvatmasamvide //

    The Nyayapravesakasutram, ed. Bhattacharya, V, Baroda, 1927, p. 1.
30. *Ibid.*, p.1.
31. Refer, Chattopadhyay, D. *Hetutattvopadesa*, 1939, p. 18.
32. Cf, *svasamanyalaksanabhyam bhinnam prameyam nastityabhyupagme* .... // *The Pramana-samuccaya*, ed. Rangaswamy Iyengar, H.R., Mysore, 1930, p.7.
33. *Cf, svalaksanavisayakam pratyaksameva / samanyalaksana-visaya-kamanumanameva / pramanantaram nasti / Ibid.*, p. 6.

34. The *Sarvadarsanasamgraha* with Gunaratna's *Tarkarahasya dipika*, p. 38.

35. Cf *mnon-sum-rtog-pa-dan bral-pa /*

min dan rigs-sogs-mi-bsres-pa'o //

The Sanskrit equivalents for these two lines are :

pratyaksam kalpanapodham

namajatyadyasamyutam // The Pramanasamuccya, ed. Rangaswamy Iyengar, H. R., 1930, p. 8.

36. Vidyabhusana, S.C., *History of Indian Logic*, p. 277.

37. Cf: *dvividhan samyagjnanam / pratyaksamanumanam ca/ The Nyayabindu*, ed. Shastri, C.S, Banaras, 1954, pp. 7 and 8.

38. Cf, *tatra kalpanapodhamabhrntam pratyaksam/ Ibid.*, p. 8.

39. Cf, *taccaturvidham/indriyajnanam/svavisayanantaravisaya-sadhakarinendriyajnanena samanantara pratyayena janitam tanmanovijnanam / sarvacittacaittanamat-masamved-anam / bhutarthabhavanaprakarsaparyanajam yogi jnanam ceti// Ibid.*, pp. 12-14.

40. *Ibid.*, p. 14

41. Cf: *rjes-dpag-rnam gnis-ran-don-ni /tshul-gsum-rtags-las-don-mthon-ba'o //*
The Pramanasamuccaya, Chapter II.

42. The *Hetutattvopadesa*, p. 4.

Also compare,

gsan-gyi-don-gyi-rjes-dpog-ni /

ran-gis-mthon-don-gsal-byed-yin //

The *Pramanasamuccya*, chapter III.

43. Cf: *tatra sadharmyena tavat/yatkrtakam tatsarvam-anityam yatha ghatadih/ drstam /*

The *Hetutattvopadesa*, p. 4.

44. *Cf: vaidharmyenapyanityatvabhave krtakatvabhavah / yathakasadi / Ibid.*, p. 4.

45. Cf: *Ibid*, p. 6

46. Cf: *Ibid*, p. 6

47. Cf: *tatra paksasiddherasiddha iti hetvabhasah //*

48. Cf: *pakse sapakse casan vipakse ca san*

(yah) sa viruddha iti hetvabhasah sadhya-viparitasiddheh //

Ibid, p. 6.

49. Cf: *sapaksa-vipaksayorubhayorbhave'bhave va samsaye vasiddha pratibandho yo hetuh so'naikantiko hetvabhasa / vadi-prati-vadibhyam sadhayitumistasyaikantenasiddheh //*

Ibid., p. 6.

Note : 1

Dr. K. Kunjunni Raja, editor, the *New Catalogus Catalogor.* (Vol.7, 1973), mentions that the elder Jitari or Jitari pada of Varendra, son of Garbhapada, flourished about 1000 A.D. He, however, accepts the date mentioned by Sankrtyayana (Refer Sanskrit Palm-leaf-Mss. in Tibet, *J.B.O.R.S.* Vol. XXI, 1935, p. 41). Dr. Kunjunni Raja opines that seven works are credited to the elder Jitari. These works are : (i) the *Jatinirakarana*, (ii) the *Dharmadharmiviniscaya*, (iii) the *Nairatmyasiddhi*, (iv) the *Balavataratarka*, (v) the *Bodhipratidesanavrtti* or the *Bodhisutrasiksakrama* (vi) the *Sugatamahavibhangakarika*, and (vii) the *Hetutattvopadesa*.

The second Jitari was a Buddhist Tantric writer of Bengal and he initiated Bodhibhagya. Fifteen works are affiliated to this younger Jitari. These are : (i) *Aparimitayurjnanavidhi,* (ii) the *Aparimitayurjnanasadhana* (iii) the *Aparimitayusstotra*, (iv) the *Candamaharosanasadhana,* (v) the *Catuhpithatattvacatuska*, (vi) the *Caturmudrasadhana*, (vii) the *Cittotpadasamadhanavidhi* and (viii) the *Dasakrodhavidyavidhi etc.* Besides, he mentions about a third Jitari (*guhya*) who was a Buddhist and the works like (i) the *Mandalavidhi* and (ii) the *Yatikarmikabhumipariskara*, also called *Adikarmikabhumipariskara*. (pp. 300-301). Thus, Dr. Kunjunni Raja mentions about three Jitaris. However, he has not mentioned the date of the second and the third ones. Sankrtyayana opines that *Nairatmyasiddhi* and the *Sahopalambhasiddhi* are the works of Jitari on Logic Refer, Sanskrit Palm-leaf Mss. in Tibet, *J.B.O.R.S.*, Vol. XXIII, 1937, pp. 1 to 57.

Relation Between Sanskrit and Tibetan

16

Biplab Kumar Mondal

Tibetan culture, language, religion and society have been immensely influenced by the Sanskrit language and Indian Culture. Most of the Sanskrit works which are not available in their original form have been preserved in the Kanjur and Tanjur collections. Indian Pandits also have visited Tibet to propagate the teachings of Lord Buddha in the land of snow and the Tibetan Lotsabas had come to the land of Buddhism to learn Sanskrit language, Indian scripts and also to translate the Indian works in to Tibetan. There developed a good deal of intercourse between Tibet and India from seventh century A.D. to thirteen century A.D. and afterwards. Though a number of Tibetan monks and scholars visited India, studied at Nalanda, Vikramasila and other places and went back, still *Chaglo-Tsa-ba Chos rje-dpal* (Skt. Dharmasvamin) seems to be the only one among them who lefts notes about the account of India, her People, Customs and Institutions (Roerich, G., *Biography of Dharmasvamin;* page-1). Thus, the Tibetans not only have preserved our ancient valuable texts, but also they have written the history of India and Indian literature of the mediaeval period. Therefore, it is essential to focus on the Tibetan translations and other literature so that we may be able to know about the contributions made by our ancient authors. In this small paper, we have tried to give some information on this subject.

Buddhism entered into the Tibetan territory during the life time of the thirty-third king of the Tibetan Royal Empire. However, the spread of this new religion in Tibet was made by the three famous Indian Pandits viz., Padmasambhava, Santaraksita and Kamalasila. The Tibetans realized that without the knowledge of Sanskrit language and Indian scripts it is not possible to go through the Buddhist scriptures. The king Sron-btsan-gan-po, therefore, advised his minister Thon-mi Sambhota to visit India and to learn the Indian scripts and Sanskrit language. Thon-mi, after returning to Tibet, deviced the first-Tibetan scripts with 30 consonants and 4 vowels. He also translated the Sanskit texts like the *Karandavyuha* and the *Ratnamegha sutra* into Tibetan towards the last part of seventh century A.D. Bu-Ston, the thirteenth century Historian from Tibet has suggested that the form of the Tibetan alphabets were given a resemblance with the Kashmirian characters (*History of Buddhism in India and Tibet*, Trns. Obermiller, E; pp.183-184). This observation of Bu-Ston is based on the fact that Thon-mi learned the Indian alphabets from Lipikara and the Sanskrit Language from Devavidyasimha at Kashmir.

Thon-mi Sambhota also composed a grammar for the Tibetan Language consisting of eight chapters. However, at present, only the first two chapters are available. The first chapter of the Thon-mi's work is an introduction to the alphabetical systems entitled *Sum-cu-pa* and the second chapter is called the *Ta-gyi-jug-pa* (Skt. *Lingavatara*).

Tibetans not only translated the works directly from Sanskrit or Pali, but they have also translated a good number of works those were translated into Chinese earlier. The Indian scriptures were attracted the notice of the Chinese Scholars much before the Tibetan Lotsabas. Prof. Bagchi has remarked that a good number of works as many as 2184 in number as per the Japanese edition of the Chinese Buddhist Tripitaka were translated from Indian sources. Most of the translations were made in China within 10th Century A.D. However, a few of them belong to the 13th Century A.D., during the reign of the short lived Mongol dynasty, but they were translations not of Indian texts but of the Tibetan Buddhist texts. (*India and China*; p.120)

Tibetans were not only translated the Indian Buddhist and other important works into Tibetan but they have tried to give an uniformity of the translations. For this purpose, Ralpachen invited three famous Indian Pandits like Silendrabodhi, Danasila and Jinamitra to Tibet and provided two Tibetan Lotsabas, Kawa paltsek and Chogro Lu'i Gyaltsen. This team was responsible for the revision of the Buddhist Texts, which were translated earlier. The members of the team tried their best for the standardization of the technical terms *(Paribhasika sabdas*) used for translating Buddhist concepts from Sanskrit. They also composed a dictionary type work as a handbook of Buddhist Sanskrit terms alongwith their Tibetan equivalents for the succeeding translators. This text is called the *Mahavyutpatti.* Thus the first dictionary was compiled in Tibetan in the Ninth Century A.D.

The history of the translation activities in Tibet shows that the Buddhist and other non-Buddhist Sanskrit and Pali works were translated into Tibetan during three phases. The first phase of translation activities was confined within late Seventh Century A. D. to early Tenth Century A.D. The second phase of translations began only after the visit of Atisa Dipamkara. During this period, beside Sanskrit, some works were translated from Chinese and Mongolian. The third phase of the translation activities commenced after the introduction of Lamaism. The *sutras* of Panini and four commentaries on these *sutras* were translated into Tibetan in this phase.

It has been mentioned earlier that the Tibetans began the translation of Indian works much latter than the Chinese scholars, but the Tibetans made most outstanding contributions through preserving the Sanskrit texts in literal and accurate translations. Prof. Dutta remarks that "the Tibetan collection of translations of Indian texts is much larger than the Chinese. In a comparison made by Prof. Sakai Shinten between the Tibetan and Chinese versions of the Indian texts, he finds the Chinese translations are wanting in 670 texts of the Kanjur and 3452 of the Tenjur". (Vide *Buddhist Civilization in Tibet*; pp. 73-74). Thus, the Tibetan translation was better than that of the Chinese, both in accuracy and volume. Now it may be concluded that Sanskrit literature served as the mother of the Tibetan literature and knowledge of Sanskrit literature is not complete without the knowledge of Tibetan literature.

It may not be out of context here to say some words about the Kanjur and Tanjur collections and also about the independent literature.

There are Seven Sub-divisions in the Kanjur viz., *Tantra, Prajnaparamita, Ratnakuta, Avatamsaka, Sutra, Vinaya* and *Nirvana.* We have 106 volumes and 1046 treatises in these Seven Sub-divisions. Most of the *sutras* were translated during the second phase of the translation activities. Those text which were translated before the visit of Atisa, were again revised latter. The *tantras* of this collection are mainly the new *Tantras* as the Tibetans belief that those *tantras* which were translated after 11th Century A. D. are designated as the New *Tantras*. There are twenty-four volumes of works in this sub-division which contain mystical theology, instructions for preparing *mandalas,* sacrifices presented to several gods and goddesses and prayers, hymns and charms addressed to them. We find twenty-three volumes in the *Prajnaparamita* sub-division.

The works included in these volumes contain the psychological, logical and metaphysical terminology of the Buddhists, without entering into the discussions of any particular subject.

The *Ratnakuta* section has six volumes of works with the discussion on several qualities and perfections of Buddhists and Buddha's instructions. Some works have narrate the dialogue between Sakya and his disciples. These works also include the discourses of Buddha given on the *Grdhrakuta* mountain. Csoma de Koros opines that those works were translated mainly in Ninth Century A.D. The *Avatansakas* has six volumes and the treatises of this sub-division discuss the Buddhist moral doctrine and metaphysics. Several Tathagatas, their qualities, former perfections for promoting welfare of the creatures have been discussed in this section. The *Vinaya* sub-division has thirteen volumes with sixteen treatises which narrate the code of conduct for the Buddhists. The *Nirvana sutra,* which discusses the subjects like Buddha's death, lamentation of the creatures on the approaching death of Buddha, the offerings presented to Buddha and Buddha's discourses related to soul etc.

The works which have been preserved in the Tanjur collection are mostly compiled by the ancient Indian Pandits. There are eleven sub-divisions of this collection viz., *stotra, tantratika, prajnaparamita, madhyamika, sutratika, cittamatrayogacarya, abhidharma, vinaya, jatakamala, lekha* and *sadharanasastra.* These eleven sub-divisions have two hundred and twentyfive volumes comprising around three thousand and eight hundred (3786) works.

Tibetan scholars have composed some independent works which were not included in the Kanjur and Tanjur collections. These works were the result of the vast experience and wisdom of renowned scholars of various Buddhist Schools those developed in Tibet. These works have been included under the following headings : history; grammar; poetic compositions; metrical literature and lexicons; astrology; mathematics; geography and cosmology; law; political writings; music and dance; drama and arts and crafts.

The historical literature may be divided into two major aspects : secular and religious. The former mainly deals with the events in the successions of Kings and other political and social happenings and the religious history deals with the introduction, spread and development of Buddhism in the land of snow. The grammatical literature mainly include the Tibetan commentaries on the work of Thon-mi Sambhota. However, two other grammarians, beside Thon-mi, have composed their glosses on Tibetan grammar. These two works are : (a) *sMa-ba'i sGo-mtshen cha* by Drempa'i Yeshe and (b) *gNas brgyad chen-po'i rtsa-ba* by Ice khyi 'Brug. The Tibetan Lotsabas composed their commentaries on the famous Indian works like the *Kavyadarsa* and the *Meghaduta*. Tibetans not only composed commentaries on Indian works, but they also produced great Tibetan poems. The works of Sakya Pandita, Kunkhyen Longchenpa, Je Tsongkhapa, Karmapa Mikyod Dorje, Fifth Dalai Lama and Dokharpa are the popular Tibetan poems. Three Tibetan commentaries are also available on the *Chandoratnakara* by Ratnakara-santipada.

The important Tibetan Lexicographical works are the mNgon brjod Tshig-gi gTer by Sakya Pandita and Shes-Rab by Sakyapa Tendzin Gyaltshen. Three Tibetan works on Buddhist logic are known to us. These three are composed by Cha-pa choseng, Sakya Pandita and Bodong Chogle Namgyal. Some of the major commentaries on logical texts written by Tibetan authors are the works of Gyaltshab Je, Rongton, Go Rabjampa and Mipham Namgyal. There are some Indian and a large number of Tibetan works in the field of medicine. The major Indian medical texts translated into Tibetan are the

Astangahrdaya samhita by Vagbhata and the *Yogasataka* by Nagarjuna. The greatest Tibetan physicians were the junior Yuthog Yontan Gonpa (12th Century A.D.) and Yuthog senior (9th Century A.D.). The famous Desi (Tib. *Sde-srid) Sangs-rgyas rgya-mtsho* establised a medical college in Tibet in the later half of the 17th century A.D. (Shakabpa, W.D., *Tibet a Political History;* p. 137).

There is no separate traditional geographical treatise in Tibetan. However geographical and cosmological texts are contained within religious works. The texts in which geographical discussions have been done are : the *Kalacakra tantra*, *Abhidharmakosa* and the work of Kunkhyen Longchenpa. However, Tsen-po Lama composed a separate work on the geography of Tibet at a latter time. Tibetans have translated the Indian Dramas like the *Lokananda-nataka* of Chandragomin and the *Nagananda* of Harsadeva. These two have been preserved in the Tanjur collcetion. Beside, we have the information about four more Dramas composed by the Tibetan scholars. They are : (a) *gzugs-kyi Nyi-ma* (b) *Dri med kun ldan;* (c) *'gro ba bzang-mo* and (d) *Pad-ma'i tshal-gyi zlos gar.*

Thus, Tibetan scholars have not only translated the Indian works into Tibetan, but also gradually being influenced by the Indian works, they have composed their independent works on almost all the branches of learning.

Buddhist System of Education

17

Prakriti Chakraborty

It is believed that in the beginning of the humanity, education was quite unconscious. Gradually human-being learnt to study the nature for food, shelter and safety. "Man exercised the physical and mental powers to save himself from the destructive forces. The elder generation advised the youngers that what was harmful, how to get pleasure and to keep away from pain. The art of cutting, hunting, defending etc. contributed to the development of human intellect, the observation of the striking phenomena in Nature laid the foundation of man's idea of worship and religion and both increased his knowledge of the physical world. Then man learnt to rise above his brutal instincts in the family, village and society under the bounds of customs and laws. This may be the beginning of conscious education".[1]

The most potent influence on Ancient Indian education was that of the religious and social environment. In the Vedic age the influence of the priests increased as the ritual of the sacrifice became more complex. The lore of the hymns was taught by the poet priest to his offsprings or near relatives and this, may be treated as the beginning of the education. Gradually, the priestly schools were developed. It was the first duty of a student to learn the hymns of his school with accuracy. Thus the system of *vidhi* and *arthavāda* introduced.[2]

During this time it was necessary to study the six subjects, technically called the *ṣaḍ vedāngās*. From these other subjects were developed.

Home Education

The system of home education in ancient India was much more similar to the present system. The members of a family, at their leisure, kindled not only the child's love of nature but his interest in literature, by telling him stories and reading aloud to him extracts from the golden deeds of the epic heroes and heroines. The child's personality was worked and developed and his work assessed and appreciated in his treatment of nursery rhymes as well as in the reproduction of these stories.

Elementary Education

The elementary education was started with the knowledge of alphabets. It is obvious that without the knowledge of alphabets, it is not possible to pursue the study further. Kautilya remarks that "having undergone the ceremony of tonsure the student shall learn the art of writing and the scripts (*lipi*)" and after the investiture of the sacred thread he shall study the triple vedas.[3] Now it may be presumed that the students were used to learn the alphabets before the ceremony of *upanayana.* I-Tsing, the Chinese traveller observed that, during his time, the students were being educated with the scripts at the age of six years.[4] However, Yuan Chwang informs that children passed on to the study of arts and sciences at seven years of age, so that elementary education must have begun earlier.[5]

So many Buddhist scriptures mention about the subject and the system of the elementary education. The *Lalitavistara* has a chapter which is dedicated to the art of writing of the letters, their varieties and the sense of each letter. Thus, this text gives a modern system of teaching the letters, as the teacher then taught each of them in association with a sentence beginning with a letter. Again, we know from this text that there were sixtyfour kind of scripts, as the student asked the teacher that which scripts he will taught out of sixty-four varieties viz. *āsām bho upādhyāya catuḥsaṣṭilipīnām katamām tvam Śiṣyāpayiṣyasi*?

The *Śikṣā* enumerates the course of elementary education as comprising the act of writing (*lipi*), prayers (*stuti*), meanings of words and their mutual relationship (*nighaṇṭu*) and elementary grammar including terminations and tenses, declensions and inflections (*śabda*). The *Divyāvadāna* refers that pencils were used in writing the letters and the abacus was used to teach arithmetic. The abacus was called as *janitra.*

Now we would like to mention here the report of the Chinese travellers which furnish some idea about the curricula of studies carried on the monastic schools. Yuan Chwang suggests that a student should learn the alphabet followed by the *Siddhir-astu*, a primer of twelve chapters. Then began the study of five *vidyās* viz., *Śabdavidyā, Śilpasthānavidyā, Chikitsāvidyā, Hetuvidyā* and the *Ādhyātmavidyā.* I-Tsing, however, narrates the subjects in more details and we are not going to discuss these here.

Beside the *tulā* and *jantra*, the *phalaka* 'wooden writing-board' and *barṇaka* wooden pen' were used as the materials for writing the letters. We have the reference of *phalaka* in the *Lalitavistara* viz., *atha bodhisatya uragaṣāracand-anamayam lipiphalakamādāya divyārṣasuvarna-tirakam samantānaṇiratnapratyuptam visvāmitramācārayamevamāha—//.*[7] The Jataka stories have also the reference of the *phalaka*. It is interesting to mark that this *phalaka* 'black-board' also is used at present in the Indian elementary schools. Students were used to go to the schools for the education like the present system. The schools were called *lakha-śālā* or *lipi-śālā* viz., *tadā māṅgalyaśatasahasraiḥ lipiśālāmupaniyatesma*.....etc.

The medium of the instruction of the primary education in the Buddhist monasteries, was perhaps, the local dialects. Once two *bhikṣus* named Yamelu and Tekula complained before the lord that the priests corrupted the language by their own dialect and offered that they would put down the teachings in Sanskrit. However, Gautam replied—"You are not, O Bhikkhus, to put the word of Buddha into Sanskrit.....I order you to learn the word of Buddha each in his own dialect."[8] This view of Lord Buddha as described in the Chullabagga suggests that the local dialect was the medium of instruction and it is really a scientific way to educate the children in the local dialect or regional language, rather than a language which is not of their own.

Admission

In ancient India, generally education was based on Veda and most of the teachers were Brahmin by caste. But the Buddhist education was not based on *Vedas* and it was not necessary that a Brahmin will be a teacher. The Buddhist monasteries were open to all concerns and not merely for the three twice-born castes.

Regarding the qualifications to take admission in a monastery, perhaps the knowledge of scripts was required. The *Mahābagga* explains in details that who is fit to take admission in a monastery and who is not. According to that text if a student is affected with diseases then he was not permitted to take admission in a monastery.[9] Besides, one who is in the royal service, a proclaimed robber, one who has broken out of jail, a debtor, a slave, one under fifteen years of age and one who is deformed in body was also not permitted to take admission viz., *na, bhikkhave, rājabhaṭo pabbājetabbo/ na, bhikkhave, dhajabandho coro pabbājetabho/na, bhikkhave, karabhedako coro pabbājetabbo/* etc.[10]

Before the *Upasampadā* ordination, a probation (*parivāsa*) of four months was required for a student who belonged to a heretic (*titthiya*) school. If he failed to satisfy the *bhikhus* by his character and conduct during this period, the *Upasampadā* ordination was refused to him. However, there was exceptions for the fire-worshippers, the Jatilas and heretics of Śākya birth. They received the *Upasampadā* ordination directly and no *parivāsa* was imposed upon them. A person between fifteen and twenty years of age could receive only the *pabbajjā* ordination and had to wait till his twentieth year for the *Upasampādā*. The novice (*śramanera*) had to live a life of strict discipline during this period under the guidance of an *ubajjhāya*. He had to practice the ten precepts like abstinence from (a) destroying life, (b) stealing, (c) impurity, (d) lying, (e) intoxicating liquor, (f) eating at forbidden times, (g) dancing, (h) garlands and scents, (i) use high beds and (j) accepting gold or silver. He was expelled, if he violated any of the first five precepts or if he spoke against the *Buddha, dharma* or *Samgha*.

The life of a novice in the monastery was regulated by strict disciplines. Every morning, a student having chewed tooth-wood, should come to his teacher and offer him tooth-wood and put a washing-basin and a towel at the side of his seat. Then he should worship the holy image and walk around the temple. After that, he should make salutation to his teacher holding up his cloak and with clapped hands. Touching the ground with his head three times, the student should remain kneeling on the ground. Then, with bowed head and clapped hands, he enquires of the teacher, saying—"Let my Upādhyāyā be attentive, I now make enquiries whether Upādhyāyā has been well through the night, whether his body has been in perfect health, whether he is active, whether he digests his food well, whether he is ready for the morning meal?" After getting the answers from the teacher the pupil goes to salute his seniors who are in the neighbouring apartments. Afterwards he reads a portion of the scriptures, and reflects on what he has learnt.[11]

Teachings

The teachings of lord Buddha was handed down by word as this was the custom during that time. Therefore, the method of teaching at that time was chiefly oral. It is further, clear from the dialogues of Nāgasena and Milinda that teachings through questions and answers were the usual rule. Again, Buddha adopted his teachings to the need and capacity of his disciples. It was the characteristic feature of the Buddha's method of teaching that he should examine his opponents' position first. As per example, lord asked Nigrodha to ask question to him about Nigrodha's own doctrine. The method of teaching at the Nālandāmahāvihāra seems to be both tutorial and professional. All the students were bound to attend the discourses without fail. The students were engaged from morning to night in discussions. The old and the young ones mutually help one another. Learned personalities from different cities were used to come to remove the doubts of the students.

The study of medicine at Taxila seems to have had both theoretical and practical course. The practical course, perhaps, included a first-hand study of plants to find out their medicinal values Jivaka was sent to Taxila for medical studies by prince Abhaya. Having proficiency in treatment he was asked by the teacher to bring something which is not medicinal. Jivaka travelled a *yojana* all round Taxila and could not seen anything that was not medicinal. The Mahāvagga gives this account of Jivaka as:—"*āṇiṇḍantomhi ācariya takkasilāya samantā yojanam, na kiñci abhesajjam addasam' ti*".[12]

Female Education

Generally, the common people believe that females were not permitted to take education in the ancient India. This is not correct at all. We have many examples that women were highly qualified in the Vedic age. In the Sūtra-period also they were not only received education, they were employed in the military.[13] They also had been enrolled as students, teachers and scholars. During the time of Gautam Buddha, females had right to study the śāstras and were taught to read and write. The Lalitavistara narrates that Gautam needed a maiden who is accomplished in writing and in composing poetry who is endowed with good qualities and well-versed in the rules of the Śāstras viz.,

sā gāthalekha likhite guṇārthayuktā
yā kanyā īdṛsā bhava mama tām varethā

and

sāstre vidhijña kuśalā ganikā yathaiva
paścāt svapet prathamamulthihote caśayyāt/
maitrānuvarti akuhāpi ca mātṛbhutā
etādrśim mi nṛpate badhukām vrnĪsva//[14]

The *Mahāparinibbān-sutta* mentions that *bhikṣuṇis* should undergo two years probation before receiving the *Upasampadā* ordination, during which they would learn the Six precepts.[15] We also get information in details regarding the Samgha meant for the *bhikṣuṇis* from the *Vinaya-Piṭaka.* The *Cullavagga* has also some rules and regulations meant for *bhikṣuṇi-samgha.*[14]

According to the *Majjhimanikāya* bhikṣuṇis should not take their seat in the presence of a *bhikṣu* without the permission of the later and the former should receive instructions from the *bhikṣu* by turn.[17]

Females were not only being educated with the rules and regulations of the Buddhist religion, they were also studied the Buddhist philosophy. The *Majjhimanikāya* narrates that once Dhammadinnā was asked by Visākha to explain *Sakaya-dithi Sakayanirodhia, ariya-atthaṅgikomaggo, samkhārus, nirodhasamāpatti* and several kinḍs of *vedana*. She explained these with full satisfaction.[18] Later she was praised by the lord himself and ranked as the foremost among the sisters who could preach.[19] She also mastered the Vinaya well. Another well-educated lady named Sukkā was a great preacher and when she taught the nuns the Buddhist doctrine, everybody listened her with great attention.[20] Thus women were properly educated in the Buddhist societies in ancient India and, therefore, Dr. Law rightly opines that the gathas sung by some women and the record of the intellectual attainments of certain individual ladies prove that a fairly high standard of literacy culture was attained in feminine circles in the days of Gautam Buddha.[21]

Teachers

We came to know from the scriptures of the Hindu about six types of teachers like *guru, ācarya, upādhyāya, caraka, kathika* and *maskarini.* Among these, according to Patanjali, the term *ācārya* was used for the highest of the high teachers, to an original thinker and efficient academician. In the Buddhist tradition five types of different terms are mentioned for the teachers viz., *dahara, stavira, upādhyāya, ācārya* and *karmācārya.* Among these, 'Dahara is a small teacher, after passing ten summer retreats one becomes a *sthavira* or settled one, who could be trusted to live by himself without a supervision; but the *Upādhyāya* and *ācārya* are the most important classes of teachers'.[22]

In the Buddhist tradition, the teachers were given the status according to their qualification. 'The brother who expounds orally one treatise in the Buddhist canon, whether *Vinaya, Abhidarma* or *Sutta*, is exempted from serving under the prior; he who expounds two is invested with the outfit of a superior; he who expounds three has brethren deputed to assist him; he who expounds four has lay servants assigned to him; he who expounds five, rides on an elephant and has a surrounding retinue'.[23]

In the *Milinda-pañho* it has been stated that teachers should be careful about twentyfive qualities when they behave the students viz., *Sammā patipanne antevāsike ye ācariyānam pañcavīsati ācariyagunā/ te he guṇehi ācariyena samma patipajjitabbam//* (IV-1-8). These qualities are 'He must always keep guard over his student. He must instruct him as to sleep and as to keep himself in health. He must teach him what to cultivate and what to avoid, to share the food. He should encourage him by the words, 'be not afraid, you will gain advantage from what is taught here.' He should never indulge in foolish talk with him. He should look upon him in his heart as a son, should not teach anything partially, keep nothing secret and he should love him, never desert him in necessity and always befriend him when he goes wrong.' Like the duties of a teacher, there are ten qualities of a student. In the same text these ten are explained in details—*'dasa ime mahārāja upāsakassa upasaka guṇā'* : etc. (IV-1-9).

Relation between teacher and student

In the Buddhist tradition a student had to live for the first ten years in absolute dependence upon his teacher and he who has completed his tenth year may give a *nissaya* himself. The word *nissaya* dependence and in the monastic system it is a relation between *ācārya* and the *antevāsin*. The *antevāsin* live *'nissaya'* with regard to the *ācārya* i.e., dependant on him and the *ācārya* gives his *nissaya* to the *antevāsin* i.e., he receives him into his protection and care.[24] In other chapters of the *Mahāvagga*, *nissaya* is said also of the relation between *Upādhyāya* and *saddhivihāraka*.[25]

Later this was relaxed and competent student had to live only five years in dependence on his teacher. However, an unlearned one had to live in dependence on his teacher all his life.[26]

Above all, the relation between a teacher and a student was like father and son. In the *Mahāvagga* lord says that—"The ācārya, O bhikkhus; ought to consider the antevāsika as a son; the antevāsika ought to consider the ācārya as a father. Thus these two united by mutual reverence, confidence and communion of life, will progress, advance and reach a high stage in this doctrine and discipline."[27]

Notes and References

1. This is the view of Sri S.K. Das and we do agree with this observation of Sri Das; Refer "The Educational system of the Ancient Hindus" of Sri Das; p. 1.
2. The direction for the performance of a rite as given in the Brahamana portion of the Veda, which according to Sāyaṇa consists of two parts, 1. *Vidhi* means 'precepts or commandmǎents' e.g., *Yajeta* he ought to sacrifice', Kuryat 'he ought to perform'; 2. *arthavāda* means 'explanatory statements' as to the origin of rites and use of the mantras, mixed up with legends and illustrations : Refer the *Sanskrit-English Dictionary* of M. William, Indian Reprint, Madras, 1987, p. 968.
3. Refer the *Arthaśāstra* of Kauṭilya, translated by R. Syama Sastri, pp. 10-11.
4. Vide : Das, S.K., *Educational System of the Ancient Hindus*, Calcutta, 1930, p. 32.
5. *Ibid*, p. 33.
6. *The Lalitavistara*, ed. by P.L. Vaidya, Darbhanga, 1958, pp. 88-89.
7. *Ibid*. p. 88.

8. Cf. *na, bhikkhave, buddhavacanam chanaso aropetabbam/ yo āropeyya, āpatti dukkaṭassa.......etc./ The Cullavagga*, Ed. by J. Kashyap, 1956, p. 229.

9. Cf: na bhikkhave, pañcahi abādhehi phuṭṭho pabbājetabbo/ The *Mahāvagga*, ed. J. Kashyap, 1956, p. 77.

10. *The Mahāvagga*, ed. J. Kashyap, 1956, pp. 78-80.

11. Refer the report of I. Tsing, translated by Takakasu, pp. 116-117.

12. *The Mahāvagga*, ed. J. Kashyap, 1856, p. 288.

13. Refer, Dash, N.K., *Education in Ancient South Asia as known* from Pānini, the Asian Studies, Vol. 6, No. 4, 1988, pp. 1-8.

14. *The Lalitavistara*, ed. by P.L. Vaidya, Darbhanga, 1958, pp. 97-98.

15. Refer the *Vinayapitaka* II/253-55.

16. Refer the *Cullavagga* Chapter X i.e., *the bhikkhunikhandhakam*, ed. by J. Kashyap, 1953, pp. 373-405.

17. Refer the *Nandakovadasuttam in the Majjhimanikāya*, ed. J. Kashyap, 1958, pp. 361-375.

    Cf, *Kassa nu kho, ananda, ajja pariyāyo*

    bhikkhunio ovaditum pariyāyena'ti?

    Ibid, p. 361.

18. Refer the Cullavedallam suttam in the Majjhimanikāya, *Ibid*, pp. 369-376.

    Cf,......*bhagavā visākham upāsakam etadavoca*—"paṇḍita, Visākha, dhammadinna bhikṣuni, mahapanna, visākha, dhammadinna bhikṣuni// (*Ibid*, p. 376).

19. Refer the Paramatthadipanī, Dharmapala's Commentary on Therigātha, XII, ed. by Muller, E., London, 1893, pp. 15-20.

20. *Ibid*, pp. 57-61.

21. Refer, Law, B.C., *Women in Buddhist Literature*, 1981 (reprint), pp. 61-62. Also refer the Chapter V.

22. According to the view of Rhys Davids and Hermann Oldenberg it is very difficult to draw a sharp line of distinction between acārya and upādhyāya. (Note 2 on I, 32.1 of the *Mahāvagga*).

Refer The Vinaya Texts (Sacred Book of the East Series, Vol. XIII). ed. by T.w. Rhys Davids and H. Oldenberg, pt. 1, Indian reprint 1968, p. 178.

23. Vide, Das, S.K., *The Educational System of the Ancient Hindus*, Calcutta, 1930, p. 157.

24. *The Mahāvagga* I. 32. 8, note I on page 179 by Rhys Davids and H. Oldenberg.

25. *Ibid*, p. 179.

26. Cf, "In consequence of that and on his occasion the Blessed One, after having delivered a religious discourse, thus addressed the Bhikkhus : 'I prescribe, O Bhikkus, that a learned, competent Bhikkhu lives five years in dependence (on his ācārya and Upādhyāya), an unlearned one all his life". *Ibid*, p. 207.

27. *Ibid*, p. 179.

The Ran-Bshin Gsum-la 'Jug-Pa'i Sgrub-pa of Arya Nagarjuna : A Critical Study

18

Lalita Chakraborty

It is believed that Buddhism entered into Tibetan territory through China and Nepal in the mid-seventh century A.D.; but the actual spread of Buddhism in the land of snow began only after the arrival of three famous Indian scholars named Śantarakṣita, Padmasambhava and Kamalaśīla in English century A.D. After the spread of Buddhism in Tibet, the local intellectuals became very much interested to learn Indian language (Tib. *rgya-gar skad*) and Buddhist Religion and Philosophy. To fulfil the want of the scholars, the Tibetan kings invited great Indian Buddhist scholars to Tibet and also, they deputed the interested scholars to India to learn the language, Religion and Philosophy. It was not possible to understand the Buddhist work as those were written either in Sanskrit of Pali. Therefore, they took the help of the Indian scholars to translate the works into Tibetan. Gradually, three thousand five hundred and thirty five Indian works (Buddhist and other non-Buddhist) were translated into Tibetan by the joint effort of both Indian Pandits and Tibetan *Lo-tsa-bas*. After the establishment of a monastery called *Bsam-yas* toward the end of the Eighth Century A.D., a central committee of the translators, consisting of both Indian and Tibetan scholars, was installed to check all the previous translations for the standardization. This Committee was authorised even to revise the old and new works in order to attain uniformity in terminology and translation techniques. This Committee also composed a Dictionary type work, which is used till today by the translators, called the *Mahavyutpatti* (Tib. *bye-brag rtogs-byed chen-po*).

A close study on this subject suggests that the composition of the famous Indian scholars like Nāgārjuna, Rahulabhadra, Āryadeva, Chandrakīrtti, Vasubandhu, Dinnāga, Dharmakīrtti, Dharmottara, Jayānanda, Kālidāsa and Aśvaghoṣa etc. have been included in the translations and now these translations are being preserved in the collections of the Kangyur and *Bstan'gyur*.

The monograph, entitled Ran-bshin-gsum-la 'zug-pa'i sgrub-pa of Ārya Nāgārjuna (Tib. '*phags pa klu-sgrub*) is not, available in its original Sanskrit. It has been taken from the Bstan-'gyur collections. The original Sanskrit title of this work is the "*Svabhāvatraya-praveśa-siddhi*" (Ed. by Late Sujit Kumar Mukhopadhyoya; published by Visva Bharati in 1939 with its Tibetan Version and English translation. However, it is attributed to Vasubandhu).

It is a known fact that the great Buddhist Philosopher Nāgārjuna of first century A.D. established the Mādhyamika School of the Mahāyāna Buddhism, some Indian sources suggest that Rāhulabhadra was the immediate predecessor and teacher of the founder of the Mādhyamika system. Chinese and Tibetan scholars do not accept this view. They argue that Nāgārjuna and Rāhulabhadra were contemporary and the latter one was a disciple of the former. Ruegg suggests that "those who think Rāhulabhadra as the teacher of Nāgārjuna (founder of Mādhyamika system) is perhaps owing to a confusion with a later Nāgārjuna (Arya Nāgārjuna) whose master Saraha was otherwise known as Rāhulabhadra". (Refer : *A History of Indian Literature: the Literature of the Madhyamika School of Philosophy in India,* 1981, p. 105.

The founder of the Mādhyamika system may not be accepted as the author of the text under discussion. The subject matter of the text entitled—*Svabhāvatrayaprave'śa siddhi* is related to the theories of the Vijñānavāda school, but not to that of the Mādhyamika system. Three svabhāvas i.e. kalpita, paratantra and parinişpanna are the main subject matter of the present text. Thus, the work Rañ-bshingsum-la 'zug-pa'i sgrub-pa belongs to the Vijñānavāda school. There is also another work entitled *Trisvabhāvan-rdesh* (Tib. *Ran-bhshin-gsum-la-nes-parbstan-pa*) which deals with the same subject that is found in the *Svabhāvatrayapraveśasiddhi* of Ārya Nāgārjuna. Some scholars believed that both the works are identical and have been written by an identical author as : "This work has two translations. Both of them are fairly literal and there is only a little difference between them and the original Sanskrit text. One of these translations was made by an Indian Pandit and a Tibetan Sanskrit scholar, named Śantibhadra and Lha-btsas (Skt. *Devasūta*) respectively. The second translation was made by an Indian Pandit, named Chandrakīrti. In this translation the work has been attributed to Nāgārjuna. As this treatise deals with Yogācāra school of Philosophy, it is certain that the celebrated Nāgārjuna, the founder of the Mādhyamika school, is not its author." (S.K. Mukherjee; ***Introduction to his edition of the Trisvabhāvanirdeśa;*** 1939 p. V). Yes, the founder of the Mādhyamika school is not the author of the text; but we do not agree with the view of Mukherjee that the *Trisvabhāvanirdeśa* and the *Svabhāvatrayapraveśasiddhi* have been composed by the same and identical person. In the case of *Svabhāvatrayapraveśasiddhi*, it may be presumed that the text was prepared by the author named Ārya Nāgārjuna (Tib.. *'phags-pa klu-sgrub*) who was identical with a

Vajrayānist master, who took the same name of the founder of the Mādhyamika system. It is suggested that this Vajrayānist Ārya Nāgārjuna lived in the Seventh or at the latest in the eighth century A.D. He was also presumedly the disciple of one of the most famous Vajrayānist master, Saraha, who is also known as Rāhulabhadra.

In the colophon of this work it has been said that Chandrakīrtti (Tib. *zla-ba-grga pas*) translated the monograph into Tibetan single handed. As a native of Kashmir (Tib. Kha-chẹ'i), the translator was well versed with both, the Sanskrit and the Tibetan Language. In the history of Buddhist Philosophy we have two Chandrakīrttis. Both of them belongs to the Mahāyāna system. The earlier Chandrakīrtti hailed from South India and lived in the early Seventh century A.D. According to the *Grub mtha' shel-gyi me-long*, the translator being born and ordained at Samanta in South India, and having studied under disciple of Bhāvaviveka, including Kamalabuddhi, who was also a disciple of Buddhāpalita, he distinguished himself as a scholar of scholars and remained, for a time, a teacher at Nālandā. Though a master of all branches of knowledge, a tripiṭakācārya, he achieved special fame in propagating the doctrine of Buddhapālita; i.e. the Prāsaṅgika interpretation of Nāgārjuna's philosophy." (*A Tibetan Eye-view of Indian philosophy,* K. K. Mittal; p. 74). The second Chandrakīrtti, also known as Chandrakīrttipāda, composed the famous commentary called the Pradīopoddyotana on the Guhyasamāja. Ruegg suggests that this second Chandrakīrtti lived in he 11th century A.D. (*The Literature of the Madhyamika School of Philosophy in India,* D.S. Ruegg; p. 105).

According to the colophon of the text—*Svabhāvatrayapraveśa siddhi*, Chandrakīrtti was a Paṇḍita as well as a Bhikṣu and hailed from Kashmir. It has been earlier said that the date of this second Chandrakīrtti was 11th century A.D. It is a known fact that the translation of the Indian works were done in a large scale in Tibetan only after 8th century A.D. The date of the former Philosopher Chandrakirtti has been fixed as early Seventh century A.D. Therefore, it is not wise to identify the translator under discussion with the former one. Thus, it may be argued that the latter Chandrakirtti was the translator of the text.

Text : I have consulted the Peking and the Narthang versions of the text entitled Ran-bshin-gsum-pa zug pa'i sgrub-pa (Skt. *Savabhavatrayapraveśasiddhiḥ*) of Ārya Nāgārjuna. The text has been compared with the *Trisvabhāvanirdeśa* of Vasubandhu. The Sanskrit verses which have been reconstructed by us, are almost all follow the Sanskrit text of the *Trisvabhāvanirdeśa* (Pub. 1939).

Subject : According to the text, the phenomenal world can be judged from three aspects. These aspects are—*kalpita, paratantra* and *pariniṣpanna*. These three aspects are called here technically *svabhāva*. According to the author of the text, the appearance manifests itself from the *paratantra* or the conditioned *svabhāva*. It does not exist by itself and it is dependent upon something else, and therefore, called *paratantra* (*pratyādhīnivṛttitvāt*).

The *kalpita svabhāva* is absolutely a product of mere imagination (*kalpanāmātrabhāvataḥ*). The phenomenal world manifests itself both as knower and known and the duality of subject and object (*gnis-dag*-gis) forms the imaginary aspects, and therefore, it is called *kalpita*.

The state of Unity in which the imagined duality between subject and object merge together, that state is the *pariniṣpanna svabhāva*. It is clear from the following verse :—

tasya khyāturyathākhyānam ya sadā vidyamānatā/
neyaḥ pariniṣpannasvabhāvo' nānyathātvataḥ//

Thus, Ārya Nāgārjuna explains about the nature and work of three aspects by which the nature of the appearance can be realized. The definitions of the three *svabhāvas* given by the author in his first four verses are quite similar to that of Vasubandhu, which have been given in his *Trisvābhavanirde'sa*. After explaining about the definitions and the nature of the mentioned aspects, the author argues that due to the existence of *citta* 'mind' the appearance manifests like knower and known. It means 'duality' is nothing but the manifestation of mind. Therefore, *citta* is the only reality and it is the storehouse of consciousness (*ālayavijñānam*) and also the mind treated as of functioning consciousness (*pravṛttivijñānam*). The former aspect of the *citta* is regarded as the cause and the later aspect i.e. the *pravṛittivijñānam* has been considered as the effect *rgyu-dan-bra-bu'i dbye-ba-yis*). Further, the functioning consciousness is of seven types; viz., (a) *cakṣurvijñānam,* (b) *śrotravijñānam,* (c) *ghrāṇavijñānam*, (d) *jihvāvijñānam*, (e) *kāyavijñānam*, (f) *manovijñānam* and (g) *manaḥ*. Again the seeds of defilements (*samkliṣṭa*) and dispositions (*vāsanā*) are accumulated the *ālayavijñānam*. The storehouse of consciousness also products the sevenfold functioning consciousness. Thus, the knower and known (*mthum mthun-bya-yan-lag-gñis-'zug-phyir*) i.e. the world of appearance comes to be manifested.

According to the view of Ārya Nāgārjuna, the *svabhāvas* possess the quality of existent and also non-existent. The author explains that the *paratantra svabhāva* exists as an error (*khrul-ba'i-dnos-pos*) and at the same time it does not exist in that form as it appears (*zi-bshin-snan-ba-yod-ma-yin*). Now it may be argued that the *Paratantra svabhāva* has its existence in the phenomenal world, but in the world of absolute reality it does not exist. On the other hand, the *Kalpitasvabhāva* has no existence, but it is assumed to be real. As far as the duality is concerned, the *pariniṣpannāsvabhāva* has no existence, but it has its existence in transcending the duality (*advayatvena yaccāsti dvayasyābhāva eva ca)*.

The first two *svabhāvas* i.e. *kalpita* and the *paratantra* are the causes of impurities (*samkleṣa*); the third and the last one i.e. the *pariniṣpanna,* being the transcendental reality, is the cause of purity (*rnam-par-byan-ba'i mtshañid-ni*).

Now it may be questioned that how we will realize these three *svabhāvas*? The Author explains that one should realize these three aspects one by one. According to the author, the nature of the *paratantrasvabhāva* should be studied first. After the realisation of the nature of the *paratantra bhave,* we should proceed towards the *kalpitasvabhāva* and then to the *pariniṣpannasvabhāva*. In the third stage, one should realize that all the three aspects are *advaya* and *anabhilāpya;* viz.

trayo' pyete svabhāvāḥ hi advayānabhilāpya lakṣaṇā/
abhāvādatathābhāvāttadabhāva svabhāvataḥ //
(V. No. 26)

Again the author says that the nature of the three aspects can be judged by (a) mere study. (b) true perception (c) logic and (d) practice, viz.,

rtogs daṅ-ma-rtogs-nam-rtogs-daṇ /
nos-rtogs-'dsiṅ-pa'i-dbye-pa'i-phyir /
so-so-re-re-rari-bshin-gsum /
rnam-pa bshi-yis-dbye-bar-'dod // (T.V. No. 27)

Towards the end of his work the author explains the nature and the activities of the aspects mentioned above through a fine example. According to him, when an illusory elephant is created from wood by means of certain spell. there we have the appearance of an elephant; actually a real elephant is totally non-existent there. In this case, the imaginary aspect is the appearance of the elephant, the conditional aspect is the form of the elephant and the absolute aspect is the total absence of a real elephant, viz.

svabhāvo kalpito hastī paratantrastadākṛtiḥ/
yastatra hastyabhāvo sau parinișpanna ișyate //
(V. No. 28)

When there is no spell, the elephant is not seen there and its form also vanishes; but only the piece of wood (the reality or *tathatā*) remains. Like this, when the mind or *citta* attains the stage of pure consciousness, the known disappears. By the disappearance of the known, the knower also vanishes. Through the non-perception of these two i.e. knower and known, the essence of supreme reality (*dharmadhātu*) is realized. According to Nāgārjuna, this is the way to achieve *vibhutva*, viz.

gñi-ga-la-ni-mi-dmigs-pas /
chos-kyi-dbyins-la-dmigs-pa-ñid /
chos-kyi-dbyins-la-dmigs-pa-yis /
'byor-pa-ñid-la-dmigs-par-'gyur // (T.V. No. 37)

Lastly the author of the text opines that having a clear knowledge about the self and others, a wise person realizes that supreme wisdom (*bodhi*), which is embodied with three essential forms like *svābhāvika, sāmbhogika* and *nairmāṇika*, viz.,

upalabdhavibhutva' sca svaparārthaprasiddhitaḥ /
prāpnotyanuttaram bodhim dhīmān kāyatrayātmikām//
(V. No. 38)

Raṅ-bshin-gsum-ia-zug pa'i-sgrub-pa-'phags-pa-kiu-sgrub-kyismdsad pa-bshugs-so//

Raṅ-bshin gsum-la-zug-pa'i-sgrub-pa (=*svabhāva-traya-praveśasiddhiḥ*) phags-pa (=Ārya) klu-sgrub-kyis-mdsub-pa-bshugs-so (=nāgārjunena likhitaḥ).

Skt. Svabhāvatraya-praveśa-siddhiḥ-ārya-nāgārjunena likhitaḥ/

Eng. The work entitled the Svabhāvatrayapraveśa-siddhiḥ has been composed by Ārya Nāgārjuna

regya gar-skad-du / sva-bhā-wa-traya-pra-be-śa-si-ddhi / bod-skad-du / Raṅ-bshin-gsum-la-'zug-pa'i-sgrub-pa / s-nas-rgyasla-phyag-' tshal-lo//

raga-gar-skod-du (=bhāratabhāśayām / saṁskṛtabḥāṣā-yām) sva-bhā-wa-tra-ya-pra-be-śa-siddhi (=svabhāva-traya-praveśa-siddhiḥ) bod-skod-du (=bhotābhāṣāyām) rañ-bshin-gsum-la-'gug-pa'i-sgrub-pa (=svabhāvatraya praveśa-siddhi) sṅas-rgyas-la-phyag-'tshal-lo (=buddhāya namaḥ) //

Skt. Bhāratabhāṣāyam (samskṛtabhāṣāyām vā) svabhāva-trayapraveśasiddhi / Buddhāya namaḥ //

Eng. Like in the Sanskrit the text is called *svabhāvatrayapraves'a siddhi* in the Tibetan language. (At the beginning of the work the author salutes Lord Buddha to complete his work smoothly).

Kun-brtags-daṅ-ni-gshaṅ-dbarṇ-darṅ/
yoṅs-su-grub-pa-ñid-kyaṅ-ni /
brtan-pa-rnams-kyi-raṅ-bshin-gsum /
śes-bya-zab-par-' dod--pa-yin //1

Kunbrtags (=kalpitaḥ) daṅ (=evam/ca) ni-gshaṅ-dbaṅ (=paratantraḥ) daṅ (=ca) / yoṅs-su-grub-pa (=pariniṣpannaḥ) ñid-kyaṅ-ni c=eva ca) /brtan-pa-rnams-kyi (=dhirāṇām) raṅ-bshin-gsum (=svabhāvatrayam) / śes-bya (=jñeyam) zab-par (=gambhiraḥ) dod-pa-yin (=*iṣyate*) //

Skt. Kalpitaḥ, paratantra-stathā pariniṣpannaśca dhīrāṇām svabhava-trayam gambhirajñeyamiṣyate//

Skt. Verse (V.V.)

Kalpitaḥ paratantraśca parinişpanna eva ca /
trayaḥ svabhāva dhīrāṇām gambhirajñeyamişyate //

Eng. The three aspects like *kalpitaḥ, paratantraḥ* and *parinispannaḥ* should be known by the wise persons.

gaṅ-snaṅ-de-ni-gshan-dbaṅ-yin /
ji-lton-snaṅ-ba-brtags-de /
rkyen-la'jug-par-dbaṅ-phyir-daṅ /
brtags-pa'i-dṅos-po-tsam-phyir-ro //2

gaṅ-snan (=yad-khyāti) de-ni-gshan dbaṅ-yin (=asau paratantraḥ-asti) ji-ltar (=yathā) snaṅ-ba (=khyāti) brtags de (=kalpitaḥ tad/ rkyen-la' jug-per-dbaṅ-phyir-daṅ (=pratyayādhīnavṛttitvāt)/ brtags-pa' i-dṅos-po-tsam-phyir-ro (kalpanāmātrabhāvataḥ) //

Skt. Yat-khyāti asau paratantraḥ / yathā khyāti tad kalpitaḥ/ prat-yayṛdhīnavṛttitvāt / kalpanā mātrābhavataḥ / yatkhyāti paratantra asau pratyayādhinavṛittitvāt, yathā khyāti tad kalpitaḥ, kalpanā mātrabhāvataḥ //

S.V. *Yatkhyāti paratantro' sau yathā khyāti sa kalpitaḥ /*
pratyayādhīnṛititvātalpanāmatrabhāvataḥ //

Eng. That which manifests itself is called the *parantantraḥ*, the form in which it manifests itself is called the *kalpitaḥ*. It is called *paratantraḥ* because it is dependant on its causes, and *kalpitaḥ* is absolutely a product of mere imaginations.

de-yi-snaṅ-ba-ji-bshin-snaṅ /
rtag-tu-med-pa-ñid-gaṅ-ni /
gshan-du-mi' gyun-phyin-ñid de /
yoṅs-su-grub-raṅ-bshin-śes-par-byā //3

de-yi-snaṅ-ba (=tasya-khyātuḥ) ji-bshin (=yathā) snan (=ākhyānam) /rtag-tu (=sadā) med-pe-ñed (avidyamānatā) gaṅni-(=yā/yat) gshan-du-mi-'gyur-phyir-ñid (=ananyathātvastaḥ) de (=sa)/yoṅs-su-grub (=parinispannaḥ) raṅ-bshin (=savabhāvaḥ) śes-par-bya (=vijñe-yaḥ/jñeyaḥ) //

Skt. tasya khyātiryathākhyānam yā sadā avidyamānā jñeyaḥ sa parinispannasvabhāvo nanyathātvataḥ /

S.V. *tsayakhyatayāthākhyanam yā sadā avidyamānatā/ jñeyaḥ sa parinispavnasvabhāvo nanyathātvataḥ //*

Eng. The *pariṅispannaḥ* should be understood as the 'never-existingness (*sadā-avidynamānatā*) of the form in which the appearance manifests itself. It is termed so as it never becomes otherwise.

de-la-snañ-yod-min-rtog /
ji-ltara-snaṅ-ba-gñis-dag-gis /
de-yi-med ñid-gaṅ-de-yis /
de-ru-gñis-med-cjhos-ñid-gañ//4

de-la (=tatra) ci (=kim) snañ-yod-min rtog (=khyāti-asatkalpaḥ khyātyasatkalpaḥ) / ji-Itar (=katham) snaṅ-ba (=khyāti) gñis-dag-gis (=dvayātmanā) / de-yi-(=tasya) med-ñid (=nāstitā) gaṅ (ka) de-yis (=tena) / de-ru (=tatra) gñis-med-chos-nid (=advayadharmatā) gaṅ (=ya)//

Skt. tatra kim khyāti? asatkalpaḥ, katham khyāti? dvayātmanā/
tasya ka nastitā tena yā tatrādvayadharmatā/

S.V. *tatara kim khyātyasatkalpaḥ katham khyāti dvyātmanā/ tasya kā nāstitā tena yā tatrādvayadharmatā //*

Eng. (In this verse the author explains that) *asatkalpa* "that which has in it unreal conception" manifests itself (*khyāti*) and it manifests in the form of duality (*dvayatmanā*). Again the non-dual aspects of that which manifests itself in dual form proves the non-existence of that form in which the appearance manifests itself.

sems-de-de-mu-yod-min-ntog /
gaṅ phyin-de-ni-bntags-pa-yin /
je-ltar-don-ni-ntog-byed-pa /
de-dshin śih-tu-yod-ma-yin //5

sems (=cittam) de (=tat) ru (=tatra) yod-min-rtog (=asatkalpa) gam-phyir (=yataḥ) de-ni-brtags-pa-yin (=tat hi kalpyate) / je-ltar (=yatha) don-ni-(=artham) rtog-byed-pa (=kalpayati) / de-bshin (=tatha) śin-tu (=atyantam) yod-mayin (=na vidyate) //

Skt. asatkalpas-tatra-tac-cittam, yataḥ tat hi kalpyate /
yathā artham kalpayati, tatḥā atyantam na vidyate //

S.V. *asatkalpotra kaścittam yatastena hi kalpyate/*
yathā ca kalpayatyartham tathātyantam na viyate//

Eng. The mind (cittam) is that which has in it unreal conception. It is called so because it imagines, and an object never exists in form in which it (cittam) imagines the object.

rgyu-daṅ-' bnas-bu't-dbye ba-yis /.
sems-de-rnam-pa-gñis-su-' dod /
kun-bshi-rnam-par-śes-gaṅ-daṅ /
jug-pa-shes-bya-rnam-bdun-pa'o//6

rgyu-daṅ (=hetu ca) 'bras-bu'i-dbye-ba-yis (=phalabhāgena)/ sems (=cittam) de (=tat rnam-pa-gñis-su' dod (=dvividhamiṣyate) / kun-bshi (=ālayam) rnam-par (=prakāram / ākhyam) śes (=vijñā-nam) gaṅ (=yat) daṅ (=ca) / 'jug-pa (=pravṛtti) shes-bya (=ākh-yam) rnam-bdun-pa' o (=saptadhā)//

Skt. tad-hetu-phala-bhāgena ca cittam dvividhamiṣyate
ālayākhyam vijñānam. yat pravṛtti ākhyam saptadhā ca/

S.V. *taddhetuphalabhāvena cittam dvividhamisyate /*
yadālayākhyam vijñānam pravṛttyākhyāñca saptadhā /

Eng. The mind (*cittam*) regarded as cause and effect is taken in its two aspects : (i) as what is called the store-house of consciousness (ālayavijñānam) and (ii) as what is called the functioning consciousness (pravṛttivijñānam), which has seven forms.

kun-nas-ñons moṅs bga-chags-kyi /
sa bon-bsags-phyir-sems brjod de /
rna-śes-lṅa-po-gshan-ma-yin /
sna-tshogs-rnam-pa' jug-phyir-ro //7

kun-nas-ñon-moṅs (=saṁkleśaḥ) bga-chags-kyi (=vāsanāyāḥ) / sa-bon (=bījam) (=vāsanābījam) bsags (=cita) phyir (=tvāt) sems (=cittam) brijod-de (ucyate) ((=citatvāccittamucyate)) / rnam-ses-lṅa po (=vijñānam pañcakam) gshan-ma-yin (=anyat)/ sna-tshogs-rnam-po (=citrākāra) jug-phyir-ro (=pravṛttitvāt) //

Skt. saṃkleśavāsanābījaiścitatvāt cittamucyate/
vijñānapaṅcakañ cānyat citrākārapravṛattitaḥ //

S.V. *sāṁkjeśavasanābījaiścitatvāccittamucyate /*
vijñānapañcokāñcānyat citrākāra-pravṛttitaḥ //

Eng. As the seeds of defilements and dispositions are accumulated (*cita*) here it is called *cittam* "store-consciousness". And the five-vijñānas are also called *cittam* as they act in various (*citra*) ways.

yaṅ-dag-ma-yin-kun-rtog-gaṅ /
de ni bsdus-par rnam-gsum-' dod /
rnam-smin-de-bshin-mtshan-ma-can /
so-sor-snaṅ-ba-gshan-ma'o //8

Yaṅ-dag ma-yin-kun-rtog (=abhūtakalpaḥ) gaṅ (=yat) / de-ni (=tat) bsdus-par (=samāsataḥ) rnam-gsum-'dod / (=trividham-iṣyate) / rnam-smin (=vaipākikaḥ) de-bshin

(=tathā) mtshan-ma-can (=naimittikaḥ) / so-sor-snaṅ-ba (=prātibhāsikam) gshan-ma'o (=anyam) //

Skt : yat abhūtakalpa. tat samāsato trividhamiṣyate / vaipākika-stathā naimittikaḥ anyam prātibhāsikam //

S.V. *samāsato 'bhūtakalpaḥ sa caiṣa trividho mataḥ / vaipākikastathā naimittiko 'anyaḥ prātibhāsikaḥ //*

Eng. In short, *abhūtakalpaḥ* "that which has in it unreal conception" is of three kinds; viz., the causative (vaipākika). the contigent (naimittika) and the illusive (prātibhāsika)

daṅ-po'i-rtsa-ba't-rnam-śes-te /
gaṅ-phir-rnam-smin-bdag ñid-do /
jug pa'i-rnom-śes-phan-tshum mthoṅ /
mthoṅ-bya-yan-lag-gñis-'jug-phyir //9

dan-po'i-rtsa-ba'i-rnam-ses-te-(prathamo mulavijñānam), gaṅ-phyir (=yataḥ) rnam-smin-bdag-ñid-do (=vipākātmakam), 'jug-pa'i-rnam-śes (=pravṛttivijñānam) phan-tshun (=anyam) mthon (=dṛśya) mthoṅ-bya-yan-lag-gñis-'jug-phyir (=dṛagaṅgadvayavṛttitah) //

Skt. *prathamo mūlavijñānam todvipākātmakām yataḥ / anyaḥ pravṛttivijñānam dṛśvadṛgaṅgadvavavṛttitaḥ //*

S.V. *prathamo mūlavijñānam tadvipākātmakam yataḥ / anyaḥ pravṛttivijñānam dṛśyadrgaṅgadvayavṛttittaḥ //*

Eng. The first is the basic consciousness. It is called so as it has called the functioning consciousness, as it has within itself the function of knowing or cognising the subject and the object both.

yod-med-phyir-daṅ-gñis-gcig-phyir /
kun-nas-ñon-moṅs-rnam-byaṅ-la /
mitshanñid-dbyer-med-phyir-zab-ñid /
raṅ-bshin-rnains-la'dod-pa-yin //10

yod-med-phyor (=sad-asat-tvād) dań-gnis-gcig-phyir (=dvaya ikatvāt), kun-nas-ñon-moñs (=saṁkleśaḥ) rnam-byań-la (=vyabadā-nam). mtshan-ñid (=lakṣaṇam) dbyer-med-phyir (=abhedatah) zab-ñid (=gabhītṛatā rań-bshin-rnams-la (=vabhāvah)' dod-pa-yin (=iṣyate)/

Skt. sad-asat-tvād dvayaikatvād saṁklesā-vyavadānam / lakṣaṇam abhedataḥ svabhavaiḥ gabhiatā iṣyate //

S.V. *sadas. attvāddvayikatvātsaṁkleśavyavadānayoḥ / lakṣaṇābhedataśceṣṭā svabhāvānām gabhīratā //*

Eng. The profoundness of the three aspects (as described in verse—8) is admitted, with reference to purities (vyavadāna) and impurities (saṁkleśa) is as much as they are both existent and non-existent, dual and non-dual and so possessed of characteristics not different from each other.

śin-tu-med-pa-ñid-dag-ni /
gań phyin-yod par-' dsin-pa-la /
de-yi (s)-kun brtags-ran-bshin-ni /
yod-dań med-pa't-mtshan-ñid-' dod //11

sin-tu-med-pa (=atyantā bhāvaḥ) ñid-dag-ni (=eva), gańphyir (=yataḥ) yod-par (=sattve)'dsin-pa-la (=gṛhyate) / de-yis (=tena) kun-brtags (=kalpitaḥ) rań-bshin-ni (=savbhāvaḥ) / yod-dań-med-pa'i-mtshan (=sad-asad-lakańam) ñid (=eva)' dod (=iṣyate) /

Skt : atyantābhāva eva, yataḥ sattve gṛhyate, tena kalpitaḥ svabhāvaḥ / sad-ast lakṣaṇam eva isyate /

S.V. *sattvena gṛhyate yasmād atyantābhāva eva ca / svabhāvaḥ kalpitastena sad-asallakṣaṇo mataḥ //*

Eng. Though it has no existence to all in reality, it is taken to be real (by the ignorants). The imaginary (*kalpitaḥ*) aspect possesses the characteristics of both existence and non-existence.

'khrul-ba'i-dnos-pos-yod-pa-la /
ñi-bshin-snaṅ-ba-yod-ma-yin /
gaṁ-phyir-gshan-dbaṅ-de-yis-ni /
yod-medmtshan-ñid-par-'dod-do //12

'khrus-ba'i-dṅos-pos (=bhrāntibhāvena) yod-pa-la (=vidyate) / ji-bshin-snaṅ-ba (=yathā-ākhyānam) yod-ma-yin (=na vidyate) / gaṅ-bhyir (=yataḥ) gsha-dbaṅ (=paratantraḥ) de-yis-ni (=tena) / yod-med-mtshan (=sadasallakṣaṇam) ñid-par (=eva) 'dod-do (=iṣyate) /

Skt. Yathā ākhyānam na vidyate, (tathā) bhrāntibhāvena vidyate/ paratantro yatastena sadasallakṣaṇamiṣyate/

S.V. *vidyate brāntibhāvena yathākhyānam na vidyate/ paratantro yatastena sadasallakṣaṇo mataḥ //*

Eng. As it exists as an error (*bhrāntibhāvena*), and as it does not exists as it appears, the relative aspect (*paratantra*) posseses the characteristics of both existence and non-existence.

gaṅ-gis-gñis-med-ñid-du-yod /
gñis-kyi-dṅos po med-pa-ñid /
de-yis-yoṅs-grub-naṅ-bṣhin-ni /
yod-med-mtshan-ñid-' dod-pa-yin //13

gaṅ-gis-gñis-med-ñid-du (=advayatvena yat) yod (=asti)/ gñis-kyi (=dvayasya) dṅos-po-med-pa (=abhāva) ñid (=eva)/ de-yis (=tena) yoṅs-gurb (=niṣpannaḥ) raṅ-bshin-ni (=svabhāva)/ yod-med-mtshan-ñid (=sad-asat-lakṣanam, eva) 'dod-pa-yin (=iṣyate) //

Skt. advayatvena yadasti, dvayasyābhāvo eva / svabhāvastena niṣpannaḥ sadasallakṣaṇam iṣyate/

S.V. *advayatvena yaccāsti dvayasyābhāva eva ca / svabhāvastena niṣpannaḥ sadasallakṣaṇo mataḥ //*

Eng. As it exists in its nature as non-dual, and also as it is characterised by the absence of duality; the Absolute aspect (*pariṇiṣpanna*) possesses the characteristics of both existence and non-existence.

brtags-pa'i-don-la-rnam-gñis-phyir /
de-yod-ma-yin-dṅos-g-cig-phyir /
kum-brtags-ran-bshin-byis-pa-rnams /
gñis-daṅ (snaṅ)-g cig-gis-bdag-ñid-dod //14

brtags-pa'-i-don-la (=kalpitārthaṁ) rnam-gnis-phyir (=dvaividhyat), de-yod-ma-yin (=tad-asattvam) dṅos-gcig-phyir' (=eka-bhāvataḥ) / kun-brtags (=kalpitaḥ) raṅ-bshin (=svabhāvaḥ) byis-pa-rnams (=balaḥ) / gñis-daṅ-gcig-gis-bdag-ñid (=dvayaikatvātmakaḥ) 'dood (=isyate) //

Skt. kalpitārtham dvaividhyāt tadasattvam ekabhāvataḥ, bālā (nām) kalpitasvabhāv dvayaikatvātmaka iṣyate //

S.V. *dvaividhyātkalpitārthasya tadasattvaikabhāvataḥ / svabhāvaḥ kalpito bālairdvayaikatvātmako mataḥ //*

Eng. As the imaginary things are all of dual nature, (as the knower and the known), and as there is (in reality) only the one chartacter of absence that (dual nature in them), the Imaginary aspect of the ignorant people has both duality and unity within itself.

gñis-kyi-dṅos-po-snaṅ-phyir-daṅ /
'khrul-pa-tsam-gyi-dṅos-gcig-phyir /
gshan-dbaṅ-shes-bya'i-raṅ-bshin-ni /
gñis-daṅ-gcig-gi-bdag-ñid-dod //15

gñis-kyi-dṅos-po (=dvayabhābaḥ) snañ-phyir-daṅ (=prakh-yānatvāt) / 'khrul-pa-tsam-gyi-dṅos-gcig-phyir (=bhrāntimātraika-bhāvataḥ) / gshan-dbaṅ (=paratantram) shes-bya'i raṅ-bshin-ni (=ākhya-sya svabāvaḥ) / gñis-daṅ-gcig-gi-bdag-ñid (=dvayaikāt-makaḥ) 'dod (=iṣyate) //

Skt. dvyabhāve (na) prakhyānatvat, āhrāntimātraika-havatah, paratantrākhyo svabhavo dvayaikatvātmako mataḥ/

S.V. *prakhyānāt dvayabhāvena bhrāntimātraikabhāvataḥ / svabhāvaḥ paratantrākhya dvyaikatvātmako mataḥ//*

Eng. As it manifests itself in the dual from (subject and object) and as it has also within itself only the one character of erroneousness, the aspect called the Relative or Conditioned has both duality and unity within itself.

gaṅ-gis-gñis-med-ñid-du-yod /
gñis-kyi-dṅos-pos-med-pa-ñid /
de-yis-yons-grub-raṅ-bshin-ni /
gñis-daṅ-gcig-gi-bdag-ñid-'dod //16

gaṅ-gis-gñis-med-ñid-du-yod (=advayatvena yad-asti) / gñis-kyi-dṅos-pos-med-pa-ñid (=dvayasya abhāva eva ca) / de-yis (=tena) yoṅs-grub (=pariniṣpannaḥ) ran-bṣhin-ni (=svabhāvaḥ) / gñis-dāṅ-gcig-gi-bdag-ñid (=dvayaikatvātmakaḥ) 'dod (=iṣyate) //

Skt. dvayatvena yadasti, dvyasyabhāva eva ca, tena pariniṣpanna savabhāva dvayaikatvātmaka iṣyate /

S.V. *advayatvena yadasti, dvayasyābhdāva eva ca / tena pariniṣpanno svabhāvo dvayaikatvātmako mataḥ//*

Eng. As there is absence of duality in it, and as non-duality lies in its very nature, the Absolute aspect has both duality and unity within itself.

kun-brtags-daṅ-ni-gshan-gyi-dbaṅ /
ñon-mon's mtshan-ñid-śes-par-bya /
rnam-par-byan-ba'i-mtshan-ñid-ni /
yoṅs-su-grub-par-'dod pa-yin //17

kun-brtags (=kalpitaḥ) dan-ni-gshan-gyi-dbaṅ (=paratantraś-ca) / ñon-moṅs-mtshan-ñid (=samkleśkṣaṅam) śes-par-bya (=jñeyam) / rnam-par-byaṅ-ba'i-mtshan-ñid-ni (=vyavadānasya lakṣaṇam) / yoṅs-su-grub-par (=parinispannaḥ) 'dod-pa-yod (=iṭaḥ)//

Skt. Kalpitaḥ paratantrasca saṁkleśalakṣaṇam jñeyam / Vyavadānasya lakṣaṇam pariniṣpanna iṣṭaḥ /

S.V. *Kalpitaḥ paratantras' ca jñeyaṁ samkleś alakṣaṇam / pariniṣpanna iṣṭastu vyavadānasya lakṣaṇam //*

Eng. The Imaginary and the Relative are to be known as samkles'alakṣaṇam "characterised by Impurities" while the Absolute is admitted to be vyavadāna-lakaṇam "characterised by purities".

gñis-kyi-raṅ-bshin-med-phyin-daṅ /
de-med-pa-yi-raṅ-bshin-phyir /
raṅ-bshin-yhoṅs-brub-kun-brtags-las /
d byer-med-mtshan-ñid-śes-par-bya //18

gñis-kyi-raṅ-bshin (=dvayasvabhāva) med (=asad) phyir-daṅ (=tvāt ca) / de-med-pa-yin (=tadabhāva) raṅ-bshin-phyir (=svabhā-taḥ)' / naṅ-bshin (=svabhāvāt) yoṅs-grub-kun-brtags-las (niṣpannam parikalpitāt) / dbyer-med (=abhinnam) mtshan-ñid (lakṣaṅam) ś'es-par-bya (=jñeyam)//

Skt. dvayasvabhāvāsadtvāt ca tadabhāva svabhāvataḥ. svabhāvāt-parikalpitāt niṣpannaḥ abhinna-lakṣaṇam jñeyam /.

S.V. *asaddvayasvabhāvattvāttadabhāvasvabhāvataḥ / svabhāvātkalpitajjñeyo niṣpanno'bhinnalakṣaṇaḥ //*

Eng. As the Imaginary aspect has got the characteristics of possessing the unreal duality, and as it has in its very nature, the absence of that (duality) the Absolute is to be known as possessing characteristics not different from the Imaginary.

gñis-med-raṅ-bshin-ñid-phyin-daṅ /
gñis-ni-med-pa't raṅ-bshin-phyir /
yoṅs-su-grub-las-kun-brtags-kyaṅ /
mtshan ñid-tha-mi-doṅ-ces-bya //19

gñis-med-raṅ-bshin-ñid-phyir (=advayatvasvabhāva tvāt) daṅ (=ca) / gñis-ni-med-pa'i-ran-bshin-phyir (=dvayābhāvasvabhāva tvāt) / yon'-su-grub-las (=parinipannāt) kun-brtags (=kalpitaḥ) kyaṅ (=ca) / mtshan-ñid (=lakṣaṇam) tha-mi-daṅ (=abhinnaḥ) cesbya (=ucyate) //

Skt. advayatvasvabhāva tvāt dvayabhāvasvabhāva tvāt ca, parinis̩ pannāt-kalpitas'ca abhinna-lakṣaṇa ucyate /

S.V. *advayatvasvabhāvātvādduayabhāvasva bhāvataḥ / niṣpannātkalpitas' caivā ucyate 'bhinnalakṣaṇaḥ //*

Eng. As the Absolute has got the nature of non-duality, and as it be known as not different in its characteristics from the Absolute.

Ji-ltar-snaṅ-ba-med-phyir-daṅ /
de-bshin-med-pa'i-raṅ-bshin-phyir /
yoṅs grub-gshan-dhaṅ-ran-bshin-las /
tha-mi-dad-pa'i-mishan-ñid-yin //20

Ji-ltar-snan-ba (=yathākhyānam) med-phyir (=asabhāv-ataṅ) daḥ (=ca) / de-bshin (=tathā) med-pa'i-ran-bshin-phyir (=asattvas-vabhāvataḥ) / yoṅ'-grub (=niṣpanna) gshan-dbaṅ (=paratantraḥ) raṅ-bshin-las (=svabhābāt) tha-mi-dad-pa'i-mtshan-ñid-yin (=abhinnalakṣaṇaḥ)/

Skt. Yathākhyānamasadbhāvat tathḥa' asattvasvabhāvataḥ / svabhāvāt-paratantraḥ niṣpanno' bhinnalakṣaṇaḥ //

S.V. *yattākhyānamasadbhāvā'tatha sattvasvabhā vataḥ / svabhāvātparatantrākhyā niṣpanno' bhinnalakṣaṇaṁ /*

Eng. As the Relative or Conditioned does not exist in the form in which it appears, and as by its very nature it is non-existent in that form, the Absolute is not different in its characteristics from the nature of that which is called the Relative or Conditioned.

gñis med-raṅ-bshin-nid-phyir-doṅ /
ji-bshin-snaṅ ba-dṅos-med-phyir /
yoṅs-su-grub-las-gshan-dbaṅ yoṅ /
dbyer-med-mtshan-ñid sles-par byā //21

gñis-med-raṅ-bshin-ñid-phyir (=asaddvayasvabhāvatvād) dañ (=ca) /ji-bshin-snoṅ-ba (=yathākhyāna) dṅos-med-phyir (=asvabhāvataḥ) / yoṅ's-su-grab-las (niṣpannāt) gshan-dbaṅ (paratantrah) yaṅ (=api) / dbyer-med-mtshan-ñid (=abhinnalakṣaṇaḥ) sles-par-bya (=vijñeya) //

Skt. asaddvayasvabhāvatvād ca yathākhyāna asvabhāvataḥ, niṣpannāt

paratantro'pi abhinnalakṣano vijñeyah /

S.V. : *asaddvayasvabhavatvādyathākhyānasvabhāvataḥ / niṣpannātparatantro' pī vijñeyo' bhinnalakṣaṇaḥ* //

Eng. As the very nature of the Absolute is characterised by the absence of duality (subject and object) and as its nature is also not such as it appears, the Relative is not to be known as different in its characteristics from the nature of the Absolute.

tha-sñad-gtso bor-byas-phyir-daṅ /
de-'jug gtso bor byas pa't-phyir /
rim-pa't-raṅ-bshin raṅ bshin-gyi //
slob-pa't-ched du-brjod-pa-yin //22

tha-sñad (=vyavahāraḥ) gtso-bor-byas-phyir-daṅ (=adhikārataḥ) / de-'jug (=tat-praveśaḥ) gtso-bor-byas-pa'i-phyir (=adhikāratvāt) / rim-pa'i-raṅ. bshin (=kramabhāvaḥ) raṅ-bshin-gyi (=svabhāvasya) / slob-pa'i-ched-du (vyutpatyartham) brjod-pa-yin (=vidhīyate) //

Skt. vyavahārādhikārataḥ, tatpraveśādhikāratvāt, svabhāvasya kramabhāvaḥ vyutpatyartham vidhiyate /

S.V. *kramabhāvaḥ svabhāvānām vyavahārādhikārataḥ / tat-prave śādhikārāacca vyutpattyartham vidhīyate //*

Eng. The nature of these three aspects (*svabhāvānām*) is from the pragmatic standpoint; it is also useful for the purpose of comprehending their ultimate nature, when viewed deeply from the standpoint of this nature.

tha-sñad brd'-ñid-kun-brtags-daṅ /
tha-sñad-byed-pa'i-bdag-ñid gshan /
tha-sñad-kun-nas-cha-byed-pa-'i /
raṅ-bshin-gshan-ma-byed-pa-yin //23

tha-sḍad-brd'-ñid (=vyavahārātmā) kun-brtags-daṅ (kalpitaḥ)/ tha-sñad-byed-pa'i (=vyavahatṛḥ) bdag-ñid (=ātmakaḥ) gshan (=aparaḥ)/

tha-sñad-kun-nas-cha-byed-pa'raṅ-bshin (=vyavahāra-samu-cchedasvabhāvaḥ) gshan-pa (=anyaḥ) 'dod-pa-yin (=iṣyate)//

Skt. vyavahārātmā kalpitaḥ, vyavhḥrttrātmako'aparaḥ / vyavahāra-samucchedasvabhāvo'anya iṣyate /

S.V. *kalpita vyavahārātmā vyavaharttrātmako'paraḥ / vyavahārasamucchedasvabhavaścanya isyate //*

Eng. The Imaginary aspect has a pragmatic nature, but that which makes use of it (pragmatically) is of the other nature (Relative or Conditioned); the other (the Absolute aspect) is of the nature in which there is total absence of the pragmatic (nature).

sṅon-du-gñis-med bdag-ñid-ni /
gshan-dbaṅ-rab-tu-jug par'gyur /
de nas-de-ru-gñis-med ni /
rtog-pa-tsam-du-'jug-pa-yin //24

snon-du (=pūrvam) gñis-med-bdag-ñid-ni (=dvayabhāvatmakaḥ) / gshan-dbaṅ (=paratantraḥ) rab-tu-'jug-pan-'gyur (=praviṣyate) / de-nas (=tataḥ) de-ru (=tatra) gñis-med-ni (asadvayam) / rtog-pa-tsam-du (kalpanāmātram) 'jug-pa-yin- (=praviśyate) //

Skt. pūrvam dvaya-abhāva-ātmakaḥ, paratantrah praviśyate, tataḥ asadvayam kalpanāmātram praviśyate /

S.V. *dvayabhāvātmakaḥ pūrvam paratantraḥ pravisyate / tataḥ praviśyate tatra kalpanāmātram asapdavyam //*

Eng. At first (the Relative), which has within itself the absence of (real) duality is penetrated (to apprehend its deep nature); then the mere Imagination in which also there is non-real duality is penetrated (to apprehend its true nature).

de-nas gñis-med-dṅos pa-ni /
de-ru-yoṅs-grub-jug-pa-ste /
de-bshin-de-ñid de-bshin-du /
med daṅ yod-ces-brjod-pa yin //25

de-nas (=tataḥ) gñis-med (dvaya-abhāvaḥ) dṅos-po-ni (=bhāvaḥ)/ de-ru (tatra) yoṅs-grub (=pariniṣpannaḥ) 'jug-pa-ste (=praviśyate) / de-bshin (=tathā) de-ñid (=tadā) de-bshin-du (=asau) / med-daṅ-yod (=asti-nāsti) ces-brod-pa-yin (ucyate) //

Skt. tataḥ dvaya-abhāva, tatra pariniṣpannaḥ praviśyate/ tathā tadā asau astināsti ucyate //

S.V. *tato dvayābhādvabhāvo (pari)-niṣpanno 'tra praviśyate/ tathā hyasāveva todā astināstīti cocyate //*

Eng. After these (penentrations) the Absolute which has the positive nature of absolute absence of duality is comprehended deeply. It is then for this reason called both existent and non-existent.

raṅ-bshin gsum-ka-'di-ranms-ni /
gñis-med-brjod med-mtshan-ñi-can /
med-phyir-de-bshin-yod (med) phyin-raṇ /
de-med-pa-yi-raṅ-bshin-phyir //26

raṅ-bshin-gsum-ka-'di-rnams-ni (=svabhāvāh trayo'pi ete—trayo' pyete svabhāvāh) / gñis-me (=advaya) brjod-med (=anabhilāpya) mtshan-ñid-can (=lakṣaṇa) / med-phyir (=abhāvatvād—abhāvād) de-bshin-med-phyir-daṅ (=atathā-bhāvād)/de-med-pa-yi-raṅ-bshin-phyir (=tadabhāva-svabhāvatḥ) //

Skt. trayo'pyete svabhāvāḥ advaya-anabhilāpya lakṣaṇāḥ, abhāvad-atathābhāvād tadabhāvasvabhāvataḥ /

S.V. *trayo' pyete svabhāvā advayānabhilāpya lakṣanāḥ/ abhāvādatathābhāvād tadabhāvasvabhāvataḥ //*

Eng. All these three (aspects, mentioned above) are non-duality (*advaya*) in character and non-expressible (by mere words), absence of (dual nature), (ii) absence of the form in which they appear, and also (iii) having the positive nature of absence of (duality).

rtogs-daṅ-ma-rtogs-rnam-rtogs-daṅ /
mṅon-rtogs-'dsin-pa'i-dbye-ba'i phyir /
so-so-re-re-raṅ-bshin-gsum /
rnam-pa-ba-'i-yis-dbye-bar'-dod //27

rtogs-daṅ-ma-rtogs (=vyutapatti-avyutpattis-(a) rnam-rtogs-daṅ (=vigati)/ mṅon-rtogs (=abhisamaya/sākṣ ātvyutpattiḥ)'dsin-pa'i-dbye-ba'i-phyir (=kramataḥ gṛhyate / dhāryate) / so-so-re-re (=pṛthaktvena) raṅ-bshin-gshin-gsum (trt-svabhāvāḥ) / rnam-pa-ba'i-yis (=ākṛtyā) dbye-bar-'dod (=jñānamiśyate) /

Skt. vyutpatti-avyutpatti-vigati-abhisamayena ca kramatah prtakt-vena trisvabhavanam jnanam akṛtya isyate //

S.V. *vyutpattyāvyutpattyyāvigatyabhisamayena ca /*
pṛthaktvena svabhāvānām trayāṇām jñānamiṣyate //

Eng. The three types of nature of the phenomenal world can be judged by four ways separately. These ways are : (a) the true perception, (b) mere study, (c) logic and (d) practice.

miṅ-ni-gñis-thos-'khrul-pa-daṅ /
dbaṅ-du-ñid-ces-dbye-ba'i-phyir /
mi-brjod-gñis-med-ñon-mi-moṅs /
gcig-daṅ-du-ma'i-dbye-phyir-ro // 28

miṅ-ni (=nāma) (gñis-thos (=dvedhā śrutam) 'khrul-pa-daṅ-dban-du-ñid (=māyādhīnam) ches (=iti) dbye-ba'i-phyr (=kramataḥ) / mi-brjod (=anabhilāpya) gñis-med (=advaya) ñon-mi-moṅs (=asaṁkles'a) / gcig-daṅ (=ckam ca) du-ma'i-dbye-phyir-ro (=nānākrameṇa) or anekatvam krameṇa (ālocayāmi) //

Skt. nāma dvedhā śrutam iti kramataḥ māyādhīnam, anabhilāpya-advaya-asaṁkleśaśca /
ekatvānekatva krameṇa (ālocayiṣyāmi) //

S.V. *nāma dvedhā śrutamiti māyādhināṇca advayam /*
asaṁkleśānabhilāpye ca ekatvānekatva krameṅa//

Eng. Name is head in two way : Under maya and as indivisible. That without any impurity and not-explainable in the way of unity and diverse.

sgyu-mas-byas-pa'i-sṅgs-dboṅ-gis /
glaṅ-chen-bdag-ñid-kyi-snaṅ-bshin /
de-ru-rnam-pa-tsam-yod-de /
glaṅ-chen-rnam-pa-kun-tu-med // 29

sgyur-mas-byag-pa'i-sṅags-dbaṅ-gis (=māyākṛtam mantravaśena) / glaṅ-chen (=hastin) bdag-ñid-kyi-snan-bshin

(=atmanaḥ khyāti yathā) / de-ru (=tatra) rnam-pa (=akṛtiḥ) tsham-yod-de (=mātram asti) / glaṅ-chen (=hastin) rnam-pa (=akṛtiḥ) kun-tu-med (=sarvathā nāsti) //

Skt. māyākṛtam mantravaśena khyāti hastyātmanā yathā/ ākṛti-mātram tatra asti, hastyākṛti tu na sarvathā //

S.V. *māyākṛtam mantravaśāt-khyāti hastyātmanā yathā/ ȧkāramātram tatrāsti hastī nāsti tu sarvathā //*

Eng. When the illusary form of an elephant is made by means of spell (mantra), there only we have the appearance, but really the elephant is non-existence in all respects.

glaṅ-chen-kun-brtags-raṅ-bshin-te /
de-yi-rnms-pa-gshan-dbaṅ-yin /
de-ru-glaṅ-chen-med-pa-gaṅ /
de-ni-yoṅs-grub-' dod-pa-yin // 30

glaṅ-chen (=hastin) kun-brtags raṅ-bshin-te (=kalpita-svabhāva) / de-yi (=tasya) rnam-pa (=ākṛti) gshan-dbaṅ-yin (=paratantraḥ) / de-ru (tatra) glaṅ-chen-med-pa (=hastyabhāvah) gaṅ (yaḥ) / de-ni (=asau) yoṅs-grub (=parinispannaḥ) 'dod-pa-yin (=iṣyate) //

Skt. hastin kalpitasvabhāvaḥ tasya ākṛtih paratantraḥ, tatra yaḥ hastyabhāva asau parinişpanna iṣyate //

S.V. *svabhāvaḥ kalpita hastī paratantrastadākrtiḥ / yastatra hastyabhāvo 'sau parinișpanna iṣyate //*

Eng. The imaginary aspect is the elephant, the conditional aspect is the form of the elephant and the absolute aspect is the absence of a real elephant.

rtsa-ba-sems-las-gñis-bdag-gis /
de-bshin-yod-min-kum-brtags-snaṅ /
gñis-po-śin-tu-med-pa-ste /
de-ru-rnam-pa-tsam-yuod-do // 31

rtsa-be-sems-las (=mūlacittāt) gñis-bdag-gis (=dvayātmanā) / debshin (=tathā) yod-min-kum-brtags (asatkalpaḥ) snaṅ (=khyātiḥ) / gñis-po (=dvayam) śin-tu-med-pa-ste (=anatataḥ nāsti) / de-ru (=tatra) rnam-pa (=ākṛtiḥ) tsam (=mātram) yod-do (asti) //

Skt. tathā-asatkalpaḥ khyātiḥ mūlacittāddvayā manā / tatra dvayam antato nāsti, ākṛti-=mātrakam asti //

S.V. *asatkalpastathā khyāti mūlacittāddvāyatmanā / dvayamantato nāsti tatrāsyākṛtimātrakam //*

Eng. Similarly 'that which has in it unreal conception' (asatkalpa) appears in dual form out of the basic consciousness. The duality does not exist there at all, but there is only the semblance of it.

rtsa-ba'i rnam-śes-sṅags-bshjn-du /
de-bshin-ñid'di-śiṅ-bsh'n-'dod /
rnam-rtog-glaṅ-chen-rnam-pa-bshin /
'dod-de-glaṅ-chen-bshin gñis-so // 32

rsta-ba'i-rnam-śes (=mūlavijñānam) sṅags-bshin-du (=mantravat) / de-bshin-ñid (=tathatā) 'di (=asau) śin-bshin-'dod (=kāsṭavat asti) / rnam-rtog (=vikalpa) glaṅ-chen (=hastin) rnam-pa-bshin (=ākāravat) / dod (=iṣyate) de (=tatra) glaṅ-chen-bshin (=hastivat) gñis-so (=dvayam) //

Skt. mūlavijñānam mantravat, tathatā kāṣṭavat matā, vikalpaḥ hastyākāravad eṣṭavyaḥ tatra hastivat dvayam /

S.V. *mantravanmūlavijñānam kāṣṭhavattathatā matā / hastyākāravadeṣṭavyo vikalpo hastivaddvayam* //

Eng. The Basic Consciousness is like the spell (*mantra*); the reality is like the piece of wood; the conception (*vikalpa* i.e. conditioned aspect) is like the form of an elephant; and the duality (of subject and object) i.e. the imaginary aspect is like the elephant.

de-gñis-rtogs-pa'i dus-su-ni /
mtshan-ñid-gsum-la-dus-gcig-tu /
yoṅs-su-śes-daṅ-spoṅ-ba-daṅ /
rim-pa-ji-bshin-thob-par-'dod //33

de-gñis-rtogs-pa'i dus-su-ni (=taddvaya-prativedhe) / mtshan-ñid-gsum-la (=lakṣaṇatrayam) dus-gcig-tu (=yugapat) / yoṅs-su-śes (=parijñā) daṅ-spoṅ-ba (=prahāṇam) daṅ (=ca) / rim-pa-ji-bshin (=yathākraman) thob-par-'dod (=prāptiḥ) 'dod (=iṣyate) //

Skt. tad-dvaya-prativedhe lakṣaṇatrayam yugapat, parijñā, prahāṇam, prāptiśca tathākramam iṣṭa //

S.V. *taddvayaprativedhe yugapallakṣaṇatrayam /*
prarijñā ca prahāṇañca prāptiśceṣṭā yathākramam //

Eng. For the deep understanding of the second one (i.e. reality or the real nature of the things), the three aspects are to be taken simultaneously; (but) the comprehension (parijñā), rejection (prahāṇa) and the realization (prāpti) have to be undertaken in their corresponding order one after another.

yoṅs-śes-'di-ru-mi-dmings-pa /
spoṅ mi-snaṅ-ba-'dod-pa-yin /
dmigs-pa-dog-ni-mstshan-ma-ste /
thob par mnon-sum-bya-ba-'ṅa-de // 34

yoṅs-śes (=parijñā) 'di-ru (=atra) mi-dmigs-pa (=anupalambhaḥ) / spoṅ-mi-snaṅ-ba (=hānirakhyānam) 'dod-pa-yin (=iṣyate) / dmigs-pa-dag-ni (=upalambhaḥ) mtshan-ma-ste (=nimittam) / thog-par (=prāptiḥ) mṅon-sum-bya-ba (=sākṣātkriyā) 'ṅa (=api) de (=sā) //

Skt. atra parijnā anupalambhaḥ, hānirakhyānamiṣyate / upalambhanimittā prāptiḥ, sā-api sākṣātkriyā //